Anthem Short Revision Papers 11+ and 12+ Verbal Reasoning Book 1

John Connor and Pat Soper

ANTHEM PRESS
LONDON · NEW YORK · DELHI

Table of Contents

Introduction

The book comprises 500 questions divided into 20 tests of 25 questions. Each test includes a multiple choice answer sheet. The questions cover the types of problems found in all verbal reasoning tests.

In completing the tests, the focus should be on consolidating the best methods for approaching questions in verbal reasoning tests. The methods have been comprehensively covered in the *Anthem How to Do 11+ and 12+ Verbal Reasoning: Technique and Practice* book. Whilst in the final analysis timing is vital, at this stage knowledge of and familiarity with methods is of greater importance. Nevertheless, 15–20 minutes for each test would be an acceptable time allocation, and achieving a score of 20 correct answers an acceptable level of attainment.

Once the exercises are completed, then the next stage will be to tackle complete papers of 80 questions in 50 minutes. These complete papers are to be found in *Anthem Test Papers in 11+ and 12+ Verbal Reasoning Books*.

When answering the questions in the 20 tests, it is useful to make constant reference to the answer sheet. For example, in questions covering letter series, number series, number substitution and number relationships, if your answer is not one of those offered on the answer sheet, then obviously you need to check your workings. For instance, in working out codes, it might only be necessary to work out two or three letters rather than the whole word. Naturally, with more practice, a more effective use of the answer sheet can be achieved.

Anthem Short Revision Papers
11+ and 12+ Verbal Reasoning Book 1
Answer Sheet 1

Please select your answers by filling in the correct boxes.

Name:

1

sea	☐	water	☐
flower	☐	weed	☐
plant	☐	green	☐

2

neglect	☐	machine	☐
kilo	☐	ton	☐
car	☐	scale	☐

3

water	☐	ocean	☐
pass	☐	salt	☐
sea	☐	son	☐

4

been	☐	her	☐
time	☐	past	☐
was	☐	over	☐

5

ticket	☐	road	☐
works	☐	get	☐
tar	☐	tram	☐

6

Come and	☐
be merry	☐
the invitation	☐
invitation stated	☐

7

There was	☐
was no	☐
blame attached	☐
the driver	☐

8

The traveller	☐
traveller came	☐
came from	☐
from India	☐

9

Always cover	☐
cover your	☐
plants in	☐
frosty weather	☐

10

The first	☐
first operation	☐
operation was	☐
was unsuccessful	☐

11

W	☐
X	☐
Z	☐
U	☐
Y	☐

12

J	☐
N	☐
L	☐
M	☐
K	☐

13

R	☐
T	☐
S	☐
Q	☐
V	☐

14

M	☐
O	☐
P	☐
N	☐
Q	☐

15

LM	☐
LN	☐
KN	☐
OP	☐
NO	☐

16

mall	☐
wall	☐
male	☐
meal	☐

17

dale	☐
dear	☐
deed	☐
deal	☐

18

rare	☐
rear	☐
rate	☐
roar	☐

19

lead	☐
deal	☐
leap	☐
leaf	☐

20

role	☐
reel	☐
rile	☐
rule	☐

21

E	☐
D	☐
C	☐
B	☐

22

C	☐
E	☐
D	☐
B	☐

23

B	☐
C	☐
D	☐
E	☐

24

B	☐
E	☐
C	☐
D	☐

25

E	☐
B	☐
D	☐
C	☐

Short Revision Paper 1

In each question below, select two words – one from each set – that together make one correctly spelt word without changing the order of the letters. The word from the set on the left always comes first. Mark the correct two words on the answer sheet.

1. (sea, flower, plant)   (water, weed, green)

2. (neglect, kilo, car)   (machine, ton, scale)

3. (water, pass, sea)   (ocean, salt, son)

4. (been, time, was)   (her, past, over)

5. (ticket, works, tar)   (road, tram, get)

In each question below, a word of four letters is hidden at the end of one word and at the beginning of the next word. Mark the correct pair of words on the answer sheet.

6. "Come and be merry" the invitation stated.

7. There was no blame attached to the driver.

8. The traveller came from India.

9. Always cover your plants in frosty weather.

10. The first operation was unsuccessful.

In the following questions, find the letter that continues each series in the most sensible manner. Mark the letter on the answer sheet.

A B C D E F G H I J K L M N O P Q R S T U V W X Y Z

11. A   E   I   M   Q   _____

12. Z   W   T   Q   N   _____

13. Z   B   X   D   V   F   _____

14. M   L   N   K   O   J   _____

15. HI   IJ   JK   KL   _____

The following questions contain three pairs of words. Find the word that completes the last pair in the same way as the other two pairs. Mark the word on the answer sheet.

16. while mile   whole mole   whale _____

17. dear read   meat team   lead _____

18. lop pole   not tone   tar _____

19. tame meat   pare reap   dale _____

20. life file   rope pore   lure _____

In a code, A stands for 2, B for 4, C for 5, D for 10 and E for 30. That is, $A = 2$ $B = 4$ $C = 5$ $D = 10$ $E = 30$. Work out the following questions, and mark your answer on the answer sheet, giving your answer as a letter.

21. $A \times C$

22. $(A + B) \times C$

23. $(B \times C) + D$

24. $E \div (A + B)$

25. $2D \div B$

Anthem Short Revision Papers
11+ and 12+ Verbal Reasoning Book 1
Answer Sheet 2

Please select your answers by filling in the correct boxes.

Name:

1
RADAR ☐
RACED ☐
RAPID ☐
RANGE ☐
RADIO ☐

2
FROCK ☐
FROST ☐
FROWN ☐
FRONT ☐
FRUIT ☐

3
GRAVY ☐
GROWS ☐
GROWN ☐
GROWL ☐
GRUNT ☐

4
WOLF ☐
WOOL ☐
WORE ☐
WORK ☐
WORD ☐

5
SEE ☐
SET ☐
SEW ☐
SHY ☐
SEA ☐

6
20 ☐
25 ☐
15 ☐
10 ☐
5 ☐

7
84 ☐
90 ☐
91 ☐
95 ☐
98 ☐

8
0·5 ☐
3 ☐
1 ☐
2 ☐
0 ☐

9
40 ☐
42 ☐
44 ☐
46 ☐
48 ☐

10
2 ☐
3 ☐
4 ☐
5 ☐
6 ☐

11
L ☐
E ☐
A ☐
D ☐

12
M ☐
A ☐
I ☐
N ☐

13
N ☐
O ☐
I ☐
S ☐
Y ☐

14
H ☐
U ☐
R ☐
T ☐

15
C ☐
R ☐
E ☐
A ☐
S ☐
E ☐

16
4 ☐
6 ☐
8 ☐
10 ☐
12 ☐

17
12 ☐
16 ☐
32 ☐
48 ☐
64 ☐

18
11 ☐
13 ☐
18 ☐
21 ☐
26 ☐

19
23 ☐
46 ☐
48 ☐
62 ☐
76 ☐

20
27 ☐
36 ☐
42 ☐
45 ☐
90 ☐

21
cloudy ☐ rainy ☐
foggy ☐ clear ☐
windy ☐ misty ☐

22
quarter ☐ fraction ☐
part ☐ second ☐
third ☐ three ☐

23
cherish ☐ enjoy ☐
help ☐ love ☐
hate ☐ hinder ☐

24
convict ☐ crime ☐
prison ☐ justice ☐
court ☐ prisoner ☐

25
forgive ☐ sorrow ☐
apology ☐ sentence ☐
change ☐ pardon ☐

Short Revision Paper 2

In the questions below, the words are in code. The first word has been worked out for you. Work out the second word using the same code. The alphabet is provided to help you with these questions. Mark the newly formed word on the answer sheet.

A B C D E F G H I J K L M N O P Q R S T U V W X Y Z

1.   If the code RKCPQ represents PIANO, what does TCRKF mean?

2.   If the code TYECF represents RACED, what does HPQLV mean?

3.   If the code TQXRI represents SOUND, what does HTRAX mean?

4.   If the code QKEP represents SIGN, what does UQPF mean?

5.   If the code SBPG represents SAND, what does SFC mean?

In each question below, find the number that continues the series in the most sensible way. Mark the correct number on the answer sheet.

6.   115   95   75   55   35   ————

7.   10   21   33   46   60   75   ————

8.   64   32   16   8   4   ————

9.   2   6   12   20   30   ————

10.   28   23   18   13   8   ————

In the questions below, one letter can be moved from the first word to the second word, in order to make two new words. Apart from this, the letters must not be rearranged, and both new words must make sense. Mark the correct letter on the answer sheet.

11.   FEED   MEN

12.   MAIN   HOST

13.   NOISY   CHAR

14.   HURT   POT

15.   CREASE   HAD

In the questions below, the three numbers in each group are related in the same way. Find the number that completes the last group.

16.   18 (3) 6   15 (3) 5   24 ( ) 3

17.   8 (20) 5   6 (24) 8   8 ( ) 8

18.   9 (13) 5   7 (12) 2   8 ( ) 5

19.   12 (5) 8   28 (17) 40   32 ( ) 60

20.   15 (30) 4   21 (84) 8   15 ( ) 6

In the questions below, select the words that are closest in meaning. Choose one word from each set. Mark the correct words on the answer sheet.

21.   (cloudy, foggy, windy)   (rainy, clear, misty)

22.   (quarter, part, third)   (fraction, second, three)

23.   (cherish, help, hate)   (enjoy, love, hinder)

24.   (convict, prison, court)   (crime, justice, prisoner)

25.   (forgive, apology, change)   (sorrow, sentence, pardon)

Anthem Short Revision Papers
11+ and 12+ Verbal Reasoning Book 1
Answer Sheet 3

Please select your answers by filling in the correct boxes.

Name:

1
conflagration ☐	breeze ☐
alarm ☐	hurricane ☐
heat ☐	storm ☐

2
enormous ☐	small ☐
fragile ☐	huge ☐
weak ☐	minute ☐

3
delight ☐	joy ☐
sorrow ☐	exam ☐
smile ☐	failure ☐

4
pupil ☐	reply ☐
doubt ☐	knowledge ☐
teacher ☐	school ☐

5
day ☐	clock ☐
month ☐	hour ☐
calendar ☐	minute ☐

6
d ☐
m ☐
e ☐
t ☐
l ☐

7
t ☐
d ☐
g ☐
w ☐
n ☐

8
t ☐
m ☐
p ☐
s ☐
r ☐

9
l ☐
e ☐
b ☐
m ☐
g ☐

10
e ☐
h ☐
k ☐
p ☐
t ☐

11
slim ☐
slip ☐
prim ☐
slam ☐
limp ☐

12
stab ☐
sane ☐
seat ☐
neat ☐
beat ☐

13
idle ☐
deaf ☐
idea ☐
deal ☐
dial ☐

14
moon ☐
tons ☐
toss ☐
soon ☐
most ☐

15
tear ☐
kerb ☐
teak ☐
bare ☐
baked ☐

16
large ☐	imposing ☐
dingy ☐	rich ☐
expensive ☐	massive ☐

17
light ☐	day ☐
dark ☐	buoyant ☐
weight ☐	sun ☐

18
extended ☐	extract ☐
alter ☐	maintain ☐
intend ☐	enlarged ☐

19
begin ☐	remove ☐
collect ☐	return ☐
conclude ☐	commence ☐

20
soft ☐	fierce ☐
friendly ☐	gentle ☐
generous ☐	hostile ☐

21
RT ☐
SU ☐
HV ☐
ST ☐
SV ☐

22
UV ☐
TY ☐
UY ☐
TZ ☐
UZ ☐

23
WM ☐
WO ☐
XM ☐
PM ☐
OK ☐

24
BA ☐
BC ☐
DA ☐
DB ☐
DC ☐

25
WT ☐
WR ☐
WS ☐
QS ☐
QY ☐

Short Revision Paper 3

In the questions below, select one word from each set of brackets that will complete the sentence in the best way. Mark the correct words on the answer sheet.

1.   Fire is to (conflagration, alarm, heat) as wind is to (breeze, hurricane, storm).

2.   Tiny is to (enormous, fragile, weak) as microscopic is to (small, huge, minute).

3.   Happiness is to (delight, sorrow, smile) as success is to (joy, exam, failure).

4.   Question is to (pupil, doubt, teacher) as answer is to (reply, knowledge, school).

5.   Date is to (day, month, calendar) as time is to (clock, hour, minute).

In the following questions, the same letter must fit into both sets of brackets to complete the word in front of the brackets and begin the word after the brackets. Mark the correct letter on the answer sheet.

6.   fil ( ) amp   foo ( ) eft

7.   co ( ) ind   to ( ) ipe

8.   pas ( ) aid   kis ( ) tay

9.   cur ( ) oth   cra ( ) ath

10.   cas ( ) ar   pan ( ) rack

In the following questions, there are two sets of words. The word in the brackets on the left hand side has been formed by using some of the letters from the words either side of it. Form the missing word in the same way. Mark the newly formed word on the answer sheet.

11.   slot (slay) play   slip (   ) pram

12.   girl (tire) time   bean ( ) soot

13.   mope (open) sent   ride ( ) leaf

14.   curt (cute) sure   moss ( ) front

15.   face (cent) pant   take ( ) barb

In the questions below, select the pair of words – one from each bracket – that are closest in meaning. Mark the correct words on the answer sheet.

16.   (large, dingy, expensive)   (imposing, rich, massive)

17.   (light, dark, weight)   (day, buoyant, sun)

18.   (extended, alter, intend)   (extract, maintain, enlarged)

19.   (begin, collect, conclude)   (remove, return, commence)

20.   (soft, friendly, generous)   (fierce, gentle, hostile)

Find the letters that complete the following sentences. The alphabet is provided to help you. Mark the correct letters on the answer sheet.

A B C D E F G H I J K L M N O P Q R S T U V W X Y Z

21.   OF is to GH as PT is to _____

22.   PR is to NT as WX is to _____

23.   PO is to TN as KL is to _____

24.   HK is to IL as CB is to _____

25.   PN is to SK as TV is to _____

Anthem Short Revision Papers
11+ and 12+ Verbal Reasoning Book 1
Answer Sheet 4

Please select your answers by filling in the correct boxes.

Name:

1
- Tom ☐
- David ☐
- Harry ☐
- Fred ☐
- John ☐

2
- Tom ☐
- David ☐
- Harry ☐
- Fred ☐
- John ☐

3
- rugby ☐
- football ☐
- tennis ☐
- hockey ☐

4
- Tom ☐
- David ☐
- Harry ☐
- Fred ☐
- John ☐

5
- Tom ☐
- David ☐
- Harry ☐
- Fred ☐
- John ☐

6
- alternate ☐
- adopt ☐
- action ☐
- adjust ☐
- activate ☐

7
- ovation ☐
- cheer ☐
- clap ☐
- encourage ☐
- soothe ☐

8
- shoot ☐
- target ☐
- point ☐
- arrow ☐
- sharp ☐

9
- lottery ☐
- draw ☐
- remove ☐
- prize ☐
- ticket ☐

10
- flat ☐
- even ☐
- straight ☐
- level ☐
- consistent ☐

11
- CAPES ☐
- PEARS ☐
- CASES ☐
- SPACE ☐
- PACES ☐

12
- CAPES ☐
- PEARS ☐
- CASES ☐
- SPACE ☐
- PACES ☐

13
- CAPES ☐
- PEARS ☐
- CASES ☐
- SPACE ☐
- PACES ☐

14
- CAPES ☐
- PEARS ☐
- CASES ☐
- SPACE ☐
- PACES ☐

15
- CAPES ☐
- PEARS ☐
- CASES ☐
- SPACE ☐
- PACES ☐

16
- CUT ☐
- LOW ☐
- AFT ☐
- AFT ☐
- ALL ☐

17
- HER ☐
- LET ☐
- LAY ☐
- LEG ☐
- LED ☐

18
- EAR ☐
- EEL ☐
- ELM ☐
- EWE ☐
- EAT ☐

19
- PAN ☐
- PAT ☐
- PAR ☐
- PEA ☐
- PAD ☐

20
- AMP ☐
- ALL ☐
- ANY ☐
- ARC ☐
- AND ☐

21
- racket ☐
- game ☐
- bat ☐
- whistle ☐
- club ☐

22
- swarm ☐
- bees ☐
- herd ☐
- wolves ☐
- school ☐

23
- elm ☐
- trunk ☐
- oak ☐
- leaf ☐
- sycamore ☐

24
- sandal ☐
- sock ☐
- shoe ☐
- foot ☐
- boot ☐

25
- second ☐
- clock ☐
- minute ☐
- hour ☐
- watch ☐

Short Revision Paper 4

Tom, David, Harry, Fred and John were asked whether they enjoyed rugby, football, tennis or hockey. Only David and Fred did not like rugby. Harry, Tom and David said they liked tennis. Only one boy did not like football. Tom, Fred, and John like hockey. Fred only liked one sport. Mark the correct answers to these questions on the answer sheet.

1. Which boy enjoyed all of these activities?

2. Who liked only football and tennis?

3. Which sport does Fred enjoy?

4. Who liked all sports except for tennis?

5. Who liked all sports except hockey?

In the following questions, there are two sets of words in brackets and a list of answer choices below. You must find the word from the list of possible answers that will go equally well with both pairs of words. Mark the correct word on the answer sheet.

6. (modify convert)   (vary adapt)
    alternate   adopt   action   adjust   activate

7. (acclaim   comfort)   (applaud console)
    ovation   cheer   clap   encourage   soothe

8. (spike tip)   (aim direct)
    shoot target point arrow sharp

9. (competition attract)   (raffle extract)
    lottery   draw   remove   prize   ticket

10. (balanced equal)   (smooth identical)
    flat   even   straight   level   consistent

The following words have been put into a code. Match the correct word with each set of symbols. Mark your answer on the answer sheet.

CAPES   PEARS   CASES   SPACE   PACES

11.   % * + ! ?

12.   ! + % ? %

13.   * ? + 0 %

14.   ! + * ? %

15.   * + !? %

The following sentences have one word with three consecutive letters missing. The letters form another word. What is it? Mark the word on the answer sheet.

16.   The water was too SHOW for swimming.

17.   It is dangerous PING near the railway tracks.

18.   The farmyard was covered with FHERS.

19.   The ground was so hard the gardener's SE broke.

20.   The teacher picked a pupil at ROM.

In the following questions, two words are different from the rest. Mark the two odd ones out on the answer sheet.

21.   racket   game   bat   whistle   club

22.   swarm   bees   herd   wolves   school

23.   elm   trunk   oak   leaf   sycamore

24.   sandal   sock   shoe   foot   boot

25.   second   clock   minute   hour   watch

Anthem Short Revision Papers
11+ and 12+ Verbal Reasoning Book 1
Answer Sheet 5

Please select your answers by filling in the correct boxes.

Name:

1
- curt ☐
- cute ☐
- card ☐
- cure ☐

2
- loam ☐
- loaf ☐
- form ☐
- foam ☐

3
- stalk ☐
- still ☐
- stake ☐
- stall ☐

4
- sane ☐
- said ☐
- paid ☐
- land ☐

5
- mind ☐
- mile ☐
- mane ☐
- mint ☐

6
- PAGE ☐
- GAPE ☐
- AGES ☐
- GAPS ☐
- PARE ☐

7
- PINT ☐
- PAST ☐
- PANT ☐
- SNAP ☐
- ANTS ☐

8
- RAT ☐
- RAW ☐
- WAR ☐
- ART ☐
- SAW ☐

9
- MAP ☐
- AMP ☐
- APE ☐
- LAP ☐
- PEA ☐

10
- ARE ☐
- RAT ☐
- TEA ☐
- TAR ☐
- ART ☐

11
- 27 ☐
- 34 ☐
- 47 ☐
- 54 ☐
- 67 ☐

12
- 5 ☐
- 10 ☐
- 48 ☐
- 88 ☐
- 96 ☐

13
- 51 ☐
- 61 ☐
- 88 ☐
- 91 ☐
- 102 ☐

14
- 20 ☐
- 25 ☐
- 45 ☐
- 50 ☐
- 60 ☐

15
- 22 ☐
- 28 ☐
- 35 ☐
- 38 ☐
- 44 ☐

16
- signal ☐
- journey ☐
- station ☐
- motorway ☐
- terminus ☐
- traffic ☐

17
- calm ☐
- storm ☐
- sea ☐
- road ☐
- straight ☐
- smooth ☐

18
- phone ☐
- ears ☐
- sight ☐
- tongue ☐
- plate ☐
- nose ☐

19
- brick ☐
- window ☐
- door ☐
- snow ☐
- shelter ☐
- sledge ☐

20
- TV ☐
- watch ☐
- film ☐
- listen ☐
- disc ☐
- note ☐

21
- DRAM ☐
- DRAB ☐
- RAID ☐
- DIRT ☐
- MIND ☐

22
- REST ☐
- LEST ☐
- TEST ☐
- LOST ☐
- NOTE ☐

23
- HELM ☐
- MINE ☐
- WINE ☐
- HEWN ☐
- HEEL ☐

24
- TIDE ☐
- TOLD ☐
- TILE ☐
- GILT ☐
- TOIL ☐

25
- PART ☐
- TRAP ☐
- WAIT ☐
- RAPT ☐
- PAIR ☐

Short Revision Paper 5

The following questions contain two given words and one missing word, and the missing word differs from each of the given words by only one letter. Decipher the missing word. Mark your answer on the answer sheet.

1.	curl	2.	loam	3.	stale	4.	sand	5.	mine
	‒ ‒ ‒ ‒		‒ ‒ ‒ ‒		‒ ‒ ‒ ‒		‒ ‒ ‒ ‒		‒ ‒ ‒ ‒
	care		foal		small		pane		mist

The following questions contain three pairs of words. For each question, find the word that completes pair three in the same way as pairs one and two, and mark it on the answer sheet.

6.	LOOP	POLE	:	RASH	HARE	:	GASP	_____
7.	ADMIRE	DIRE	:	ALWAYS	LAYS	:	PAINTS	_____
8.	DWARF	RAW	:	STARE	RAT	:	STRAW	_____
9.	ASSIST	SIT	:	FRIEND	RED	:	SAMPLE	_____
10.	CANCEL	CAN	:	BANTER	TAN	:	CREATE	_____

In the following questions, the three numbers in each group are related in the same way. Given this, find the number that completes the last group, and mark it on the answer sheet.

11.	8 (18) 5	6 (26) 10	7 ( ) 20
12.	16 (2) 8	38 (19) 2	80 ( ) 8
13.	6 (34) 4	8 (82) 9	17 ( ) 3
14.	30 (19) 8	70 (45) 20	40 ( ) 10
15.	18 (29) 10	24 (28) 8	32 ( ) 6

In the following questions, find two words – one from each group – that will complete the sentence in the best way. Mark them on the answer sheet.

16. Train is to (signal, journey, station) as bus is to (motorway, terminus, traffic).

17. Rough is to (calm, storm, sea) as crooked is to (road, straight, smooth).

18. Hearing is to (phone, ears, sight) as taste is to (tongue, plate, nose).

19. House is to (brick, window, door) as igloo is to (snow, shelter, sledge).

20. DVD is to (TV, watch, film) as music is to (listen, disc, note).

In the following questions, the middle word in the first set has been formed from some of the letters in those on either side of it. Find the missing word in the second set, formed in exactly the same way as in the first. Mark the newly formed word on the answer sheet.

21. MAST (TOMB) BOAT : ARID ( ) BRIM

22. CROP (PORK) ROCK : FRET ( ) SLOT

23. FROM (ROSE) STEM : WHEN ( ) LIME

24. CORE (CART) BATH : GOLD ( ) KITE

25. CRIB (BRIM) MIRE : WASP ( ) TRIP

Anthem Short Revision Papers
11+ and 12+ Verbal Reasoning Book 1
Answer Sheet 6

Please select your answers by filling in the correct boxes.

Name:

1
K ☐
I ☐
N ☐
D ☐

2
H ☐
E ☐
A ☐
R ☐

3
F ☐
R ☐
G ☐
T ☐

4
F ☐
A ☐
I ☐
R ☐

5
P ☐
A ☐
I ☐
T ☐

6
E ☐
Y ☐
O ☐
F ☐
A ☐

7
I ☐
E ☐
H ☐
T ☐
M ☐

8
P ☐
G ☐
S ☐
E ☐
A ☐

9
S ☐
D ☐
L ☐
T ☐
W ☐

10
L ☐
R ☐
M ☐
T ☐
S ☐

11
PR ☐
QT ☐
OS ☐
PQ ☐
QR ☐

12
GJ ☐
HI ☐
HJ ☐
HK ☐
IJ ☐

13
VR ☐
WS ☐
WT ☐
WR ☐
NR ☐

14
SY ☐
SX ☐
SZ ☐
TZ ☐
VZ ☐

15
NS ☐
BE ☐
ST ☐
BD ☐
NT ☐

16
swindle ☐   defraud ☐
encourage ☐   miserable ☐
joyful ☐   comfort ☐

17
expensive ☐   treasure ☐
value ☐   cheap ☐
nourish ☐   sustain ☐

18
follow ☐   obey
command ☐   travel
encourage ☐   persuade

19
enchant ☐   displeasure ☐
miniature ☐   giant ☐
mislead ☐   trick ☐

20
pardon ☐   condemn ☐
please ☐   excuse ☐
release ☐   absolve ☐

21
The journey ☐
journey was ☐
was by ☐
bus and ☐
and rail ☐

22
The fairy ☐
decorated the ☐
the top ☐
top layer ☐
the cake ☐

23
The stolen ☐
stolen diamond ☐
diamond was ☐
was never ☐
never recovered ☐

24
The top ☐
top almost ☐
almost reaches ☐
reaches ten ☐
ten metres ☐

25
Journey of ☐
the bus ☐
bus ended ☐
ended at ☐
the terminus ☐

Short Revision Paper 6

In the following questions, one letter can be moved from the word on the left and inserted into the word on the right to make two new words. The letters must not be rearranged. Mark the correct letter on the answer sheet.

1.   KIND   OUGHT

2.   HEAR   MEN

3.   FORGET   HEM

4.   FAIR   HER

5.   PAINT   HEAR

In the following questions, you must form two new words. Find the letter that fits into the bracket, completing the word in front of it and beginning the word after it. Mark the correct letter on the answer sheet.

6.   BOD   ( )   EAR   MAN   ( )   EAST

7.   ARC   ( )   INT   HEAT ( )   ILL

8.   CLAS ( )   LUM   HIS   ( )   KID

9.   DEB   ( )   IN   FEE   ( )   HAT

10.   DUE   ( )   ASK   PEA   ( )   HERE

Find the letters that complete the following sentences. The alphabet is provided to help you. Mark the correct letters on the answer sheet.

A B C D E F G H I J K L M N O P Q R S T U V W X Y Z

11.   EF is to IJ as MN is to _____

12.   SU is to QS as JL is to _____

13.   AZ is to DW as TU is to _____

14.   KM is to HP as VW is to _____

15.   OP is to NQ as CD is to _____

In the following questions, find the two words – one from each group – that are the most opposite in meaning. Mark both words on the answer sheet.

16.   (swindle   encourage   joyful)   (defraud   miserable   comfort)

17.   (expensive   value   nourish)   (treasure   cheap   sustain)

18.   (follow   command   encourage)   (obey   travel   persuade)

19.   (enchant   miniature   mislead)   (displeasure   giant   trick)

20.   (pardon   please   release)   (condemn   excuse   absolve)

In the following questions, find a word of four letters that is hidden at the end of one word and the beginning of the next. Mark the two words on the answer sheet.

21.   The journey was by bus and rail.

22.   A fairy decorated the top layer of the cake.

23.   The stolen diamond was never recovered.

24.   The top almost reaches ten metres.

25.   The journey of the bus ended at the terminus.

Anthem Short Revision Papers
11+ and 12+ Verbal Reasoning Book 1
Answer Sheet 7

Please select your answers by filling in the correct boxes.

Name:

1
- 26 ☐
- 28 ☐
- 25 ☐
- 27 ☐
- 24 ☐

2
- 3 ☐
- 4 ☐
- 5 ☐
- 7 ☐
- 8 ☐

3
- 116 ☐
- 179 ☐
- 242 ☐
- 248 ☐
- 268 ☐

4
- 40 ☐
- 52 ☐
- 58 ☐
- 64 ☐
- 30 ☐

5
- 10 ☐
- 12 ☐
- 14 ☐
- 16 ☐
- 18 ☐

6
- UTRB ☐
- UTQC ☐
- UTQD ☐
- UTQB ☐
- USQB ☐

7
- TMFQR ☐
- TMFVU ☐
- TMFQU ☐
- TNFGU ☐
- TNFRU ☐

8
- ETLSP ☐
- ETMSP ☐
- ETNSP ☐
- ETLRP ☐
- ETLPR ☐

9
- SCRAP ☐
- SCRUB ☐
- STAIN ☐
- SCREW ☐
- SPADE ☐

10
- IZUFE ☐
- IZUDF ☐
- IZRDF ☐
- IZRTE ☐
- IZUDE ☐

11
- Tom ☐
- Jim ☐
- Harry ☐
- Tony ☐
- Fred ☐

12
- Tom ☐
- Jim ☐
- Harry ☐
- Tony ☐
- Fred ☐

13
- Tom ☐
- Jim ☐
- Harry ☐
- Tony ☐
- Fred ☐

14
- Tom ☐
- Jim ☐
- Harry ☐
- Tony ☐
- Fred ☐

15
- Tom ☐
- Jim ☐
- Harry ☐
- Tony ☐
- Fred ☐

16
- yearly ☐ | monthly ☐
- date ☐ | minute ☐
- time ☐ | annually ☐

17
- medal ☐ | bravery ☐
- valour ☐ | victory ☐
- hero ☐ | soldier ☐

18
- terror ☐ | ghost ☐
- stormy ☐ | haunted ☐
- shake ☐ | fear ☐

19
- pantomime ☐ | circus ☐
- tent ☐ | show ☐
- reveal ☐ | camping ☐

20
- doctor ☐ | cure ☐
- remedy ☐ | surgery ☐
- prescription ☐ | health ☐

21
- A ☐
- B ☐
- C ☐
- D ☐
- E ☐

22
- A ☐
- B ☐
- C ☐
- D ☐
- E ☐

23
- A ☐
- B ☐
- C ☐
- D ☐
- E ☐

24
- A ☐
- B ☐
- C ☐
- D ☐
- E ☐

25
- A ☐
- B ☐
- C ☐
- D ☐
- E ☐

Short Revision Paper 7

In each of the following questions find the number that continues the series in the best way. Mark the correct number on the answer sheet.

1.　43　38　34　31　29　————————

2.　40　2　20　2　10　2　————————

3.　5　12　27　58　121　————————

4.　246　244　122　120　60　————————

5.　70　58　44　28　————————

In the following questions, a different code is used for each question. Work out the answers marking the correct answer on the answer sheet. An alphabet is provided to help you.

A B C D E F G H I J K L M N O P Q R S T U V W X Y Z

6.　If the code for CARED is XQBTU what is the code for DEAR?

7.　If the code for THINK is UIJOL what is the code for SLEPT?

8.　If the code for COATS is DQDXX what is the code for DRINK?

9.　If the code for CRUMB is DTXQG what word is represented by TEUIB?

10.　If the code for SLIME is TKJLF what is the code for HATED?

Tom, Jim, Harry, Tony and Fred were asked whether they liked tea, coffee, milk or hot chocolate. All except Jim and Harry liked tea. All except Tom and Tony liked milk. Tom and Harry did not like coffee and only Jim did not like hot chocolate.

11.　Who liked all four drinks?

12.　Who enjoyed all four drinks, except milk?

13.　Who enjoyed only tea and chocolate?

14.　Who enjoyed only coffee and milk?

15.　Who enjoyed only milk and hot chocolate?

In the following questions, select the two words – one from each bracket – that are closest in meaning. Mark the correct two words on the answer sheet.

16.   (yearly, date, time)   (monthly, minute, annually)

17.   (medal, valour, hero)   (bravery, victory, soldier)

18.   (terror, stormy, shake)   (ghost, haunted, fear)

19.   (pantomime, tent, reveal)   (circus, show, camping)

20.   (doctor, remedy, prescription)   (cure, surgery, health)

Work out the following, in each case giving your answer as a letter. Mark the correct answer on the answer sheet.

A = 3   B = 2   C = 5   D = 6   E = 20

21. $2C - (A + B)$

22. $3D + B$

23. $D \div A$

24. $D \div (D - 2B)$

25. $BC \div (E \div 2B)$

Anthem Short Revision Papers
11+ and 12+ Verbal Reasoning Book 1
Answer Sheet 8

Please select your answers by filling in the correct boxes.

Name:

1

RAIN ☐	DARK ☐
SLEET ☐	LIGHT ☐
SUN ☐	HEAT ☐

2

DESK ☐	SILK ☐
TABLE ☐	CLOTH ☐
STOOL ☐	FELT ☐

3

ARM ☐	COAT ☐
CHEST ☐	PANTS ☐
WAIST ☐	SHIRT ☐

4

PLAY ☐	OR ☐
ACT ☐	BY ☐
SCENE ☐	TO ☐

5

TEE ☐	OBJECT ☐
NO ☐	POT ☐
DRESS ☐	THING ☐

6

| RENDER ☐ |
| REAPER ☐ |
| SENDER ☐ |
| READER ☐ |

7

| ECHO ☐ |
| CARD ☐ |
| HOSE ☐ |
| HERO ☐ |
| REAR ☐ |

8

| TEAR ☐ |
| SEAT ☐ |
| EASE ☐ |
| DATE ☐ |
| EATS ☐ |

9

| WEED ☐ |
| NEED ☐ |
| SEED ☐ |
| SEES ☐ |
| DEED ☐ |

10

| HURT ☐ |
| PERM ☐ |
| PERT ☐ |
| HATE ☐ |
| PAST ☐ |

11

| TIC ☐ |
| TIN ☐ |
| TIE ☐ |
| SIN ☐ |
| SIP ☐ |

12

| TEA ☐ |
| TEE ☐ |
| SEE ☐ |
| SEA ☐ |
| SET ☐ |

13

| RING ☐ |
| RANG ☐ |
| REIN ☐ |
| RAIN ☐ |
| RANT ☐ |

14

| SCARE ☐ |
| STORE ☐ |
| SCORE ☐ |
| SCONE ☐ |
| STONE ☐ |

15

| PAIL ☐ |
| PANT ☐ |
| PAIN ☐ |
| PAIR ☐ |
| PARE ☐ |

16

| 31 ☐ |
| 38 ☐ |
| 40 ☐ |
| 42 ☐ |
| 49 ☐ |

17

| 8 ☐ |
| 6 ☐ |
| 4 ☐ |
| 2 ☐ |
| 1 ☐ |

18

| 61 ☐ |
| 66 ☐ |
| 70 ☐ |
| 76 ☐ |
| 78 ☐ |

19

| 10 ☐ |
| 15 ☐ |
| 30 ☐ |
| 50 ☐ |
| 110 ☐ |

20

| 70 ☐ |
| 84 ☐ |
| 98 ☐ |
| 190 ☐ |
| 210 ☐ |

21

| air on ☐ |
| the hills ☐ |
| hills is ☐ |
| is refreshing ☐ |

22

| Apple pie ☐ |
| pie rarely ☐ |
| rarely is ☐ |
| is disliked ☐ |

23

| The detective ☐ |
| detective found ☐ |
| the missing ☐ |
| missing watch ☐ |

24

| Strawberries with ☐ |
| with cream ☐ |
| cream are ☐ |
| are popular ☐ |

25

| Tom races ☐ |
| races cars ☐ |
| cars for ☐ |
| a hobby ☐ |

Short Revision Paper 8

In the questions below, choose two words – one from each bracket – that will together make one correctly spelt word, without changing the order of the letters. The word from the bracket on the left always comes first. Mark the two correct words on the answer sheet.

1.   (RAIN SLEET SUN)   (DARK LIGHT HEAT)

2.   (DESK TABLE STOOL)   (SILK CLOTH FELT)

3.   (ARM CHEST WAIST)   (COAT PANTS SHIRT)

4.   (PLAY ACT SCENE)   (OR BY TO)

5.   (TEE NO DRESS)   (OBJECT POT THING)

In the questions below the words are in pairs. Mark on your answer sheet the word that completes the last pair in the same way as the other pairs in each question. The word you make must be a real word.

6.   DEAL   LEADER : DENT   TENDER : PEAR   _____

7.   CARES   SCAR   : ALLOW   WALL   : CHOSE   _____

8.   GRAVEL RAGE   : SPOKEN POSE   : SEATED _____

9.   SET   SEES   : TOO   NOON   : DEW   _____

10. GEM   GERM   : HAM   HARM   : PET   _____

In each of the following questions, the first coded word in each sentence has been worked out for you. Work out the second using the same code. The alphabet is provided to help you. Mark the newly formed word on the answer sheet.

A B C D E F G H I J K L M N O P Q R S T U V W X Y Z

11.   If DPBU stands for COAT and TIJSU stands for SHIRT what does UJF stand for?

12.   If KZJD stands for LAKE and QHUDQ stands for RIVER what does RDZ stand for?

13.   If ENQWF stands for CLOUD and ITQWPF stands for GROUND what does TCKP stand for?

14.   If ITQCP stands for GROAN what does UEQTG stand for?

15.   If GSUP stands for BORN what does UELP stand for?

In the following questions, the three numbers in each group are related in the same way. Find the number that completes the last group. Mark the correct number on the answer sheet.

16.   5 (32) 11   7 (32) 9   11 ( ) 9

17.   12 (4) 6   18 (6) 10   24 ( ) 20

18.   5 (40) 6   7 (52) 6   11 ( ) 6

19.   21 (16) 10   39 (24) 30   70 ( ) 40

20.   22 (120) 6   42 (200) 5   12 ( ) 7

In each of the following questions, there is a word hidden at the end of one word and the beginning of the next. Find the pair of words that contain the hidden word. Mark the correct pair of words on the answer sheet.

21.   The air on the hills is refreshing.

22.   Apple pie rarely is disliked.

23.   The detective found the missing watch.

24.   Strawberries with cream are popular.

25.   Tom races cars for a hobby.

Anthem Short Revision Papers
11+ and 12+ Verbal Reasoning Book 1
Answer Sheet 9

Please select your answers by filling in the correct boxes.

Name:

1

copy ☐	photograph ☐
clean ☐	cheat ☐
vague ☐	clear ☐

2

liberty ☐	prison ☐
condemn ☐	captivity ☐
blame ☐	cell ☐

3

round ☐	jar ☐
empty ☐	circular ☐
bottle ☐	full ☐

4

clean ☐	answer ☐
litter ☐	approve ☐
refuse ☐	tidy ☐

5

mountain ☐	flat ☐
steep ☐	incline ☐
valley ☐	side ☐

6

trap ☐	ocean ☐
lose ☐	edit ☐
piece ☐	water ☐

7

house ☐	property ☐
live ☐	empty ☐
rest ☐	occupied ☐

8

Greece ☐	criminal ☐
modern ☐	law ☐
building ☐	guilty ☐

9

wheel ☐	wind ☐
car ☐	ocean ☐
speed ☐	yacht ☐

10

persuade ☐	rigid ☐
stage ☐	flexible ☐
punctual ☐	still ☐

11

| 31 ☐ |
| 32 ☐ |
| 30 ☐ |
| 29 ☐ |
| 28 ☐ |

12

| 720 ☐ |
| 1080 ☐ |
| 1250 ☐ |
| 1800 ☐ |
| 2050 ☐ |

13

| 41 ☐ |
| 43 ☐ |
| 40 ☐ |
| 42 ☐ |
| 39 ☐ |

14

| 96 ☐ |
| 120 ☐ |
| 144 ☐ |
| 216 ☐ |
| 360 ☐ |

15

| 13 ☐ |
| 14 ☐ |
| 15 ☐ |
| 16 ☐ |
| 17 ☐ |

16

| P ☐ |
| L ☐ |
| A ☐ |
| N ☐ |
| T ☐ |

17

| T ☐ |
| E ☐ |
| A ☐ |
| C ☐ |
| H ☐ |

18

| P ☐ |
| O ☐ |
| S ☐ |
| T ☐ |

19

| M ☐ |
| E ☐ |
| A ☐ |
| N ☐ |

20

| F ☐ |
| O ☐ |
| U ☐ |
| R ☐ |

21

| SO ☐ |
| RP ☐ |
| ST ☐ |
| RO ☐ |
| WP ☐ |

22

| OQ ☐ |
| PR ☐ |
| PS ☐ |
| OT ☐ |
| PQ ☐ |

23

| RX ☐ |
| RW ☐ |
| SY ☐ |
| RY ☐ |
| TY ☐ |

24

| VX ☐ |
| VY ☐ |
| UZ ☐ |
| UY ☐ |
| VZ ☐ |

25

| YW ☐ |
| YZ ☐ |
| XZ ☐ |
| XX ☐ |
| YX ☐ |

Short Revision Paper 9

In the following questions, find the two words – one from each bracket – which are most opposite in meaning. Mark the correct pair of words on the answer sheet.

1.   (copy clean vague)   (photograph cheat clear)

2.   (liberty condemn blame)   (prison captivity cell)

3.   (round empty bottle)   (jar circular full)

4.   (clean litter refuse)   (answer approve tidy)

5.   (mountain steep valley)   (flat incline side)

In the following questions, select two words – one from each bracket – which complete the sentence in the best way. Mark the correct pair of words on the answer sheet.

6.   Part is to (trap, lose, piece) as tide is to (ocean, edit, water).

7.   Residence is to (house, live, rest) as vacant is to (property, empty, occupied).

8.   Ancient is to (Greece, modern, building) as innocent is to (criminal, law, guilty).

9.   Engine is to (wheel, car, speed) as sail is to (wind, ocean, yacht).

10. Prompt is to (persuade, stage, punctual) as stiff is to (rigid, flexible, still).

In the following questions, complete the number series. Mark the correct number on the answer sheet.

11. 44 43 41 38 34 _____

12. 3 18 90 360 _____

13. 60 58 55 51 46 _____

14. 6 8 12 24 24 72 48 _____

15. 90 45 46 23 24 12 _____

In the following questions, remove one letter from the word on the left and insert this letter into the word on the right, creating two new words. The letters must not be rearranged. Mark the correct letter on your answer sheet.

16.   PLANT   HERE

17.   TEACH   EAR

18.   POST   CAT

19.   MEAN   FAST

20.   FOUR   BOND

Find the pair of letters that best complete the following sentences. The alphabet is provided to help you. Mark the correct letters on the answer sheet.

A B C D E F G H I J K L M N O P Q R S T U V W X Y Z

21.   DG is to FD as PR is to ————————

22.   PT is to QS as OR is to ————————

23.   DF is to ZH as VW is to ————————

24.   MN is to KO as XY is to ————————

25.   AD is to FH as TV is to ————————

Anthem Short Revision Papers
11+ and 12+ Verbal Reasoning Book 1
Answer Sheet 10

Please select your answers by filling in the correct boxes.

Name:

1

HIGH ☐	HIVE ☐
BE ☐	TOP ☐
BELL ☐	LOW ☐

2

HIDE ☐	COVER ☐
STOP ☐	TURN ☐
OVER ☐	WALK ☐

3

DOG ☐	TRACK ☐
TRUMP ☐	BIKE ☐
CAR ☐	PET ☐

4

LIGHT ☐	FALL ☐
NIGHT ☐	DAY ☐
OUT ☐	SUN ☐

5

NECK ☐	ROUND ☐
TIE ☐	BOW ☐
KNOT ☐	LACE ☐

6

| FEND ☐ |
| FOND ☐ |
| FUND ☐ |
| FIND ☐ |

7

| JAUNT ☐ |
| JOINT ☐ |
| JETTY ☐ |
| JOLLY ☐ |

8

| RAW ☐ |
| WAG ☐ |
| WIG ☐ |
| WAR ☐ |

9

| RED ☐ |
| RID ☐ |
| RIG ☐ |
| RAM ☐ |

10

| MIRE ☐ |
| RICE ☐ |
| MICE ☐ |
| DICE ☐ |

11

plead ☐	diminish ☐
expand ☐	guilty ☐
shrink ☐	large ☐

12

happy ☐	despair ☐
elation ☐	envious ☐
jealous ☐	sad ☐

13

boast ☐	known ☐
strange ☐	handicap ☐
injure ☐	brag ☐

14

devise ☐	bravery ☐
courage ☐	part ☐
mix ☐	separate ☐

15

still ☐	reduce ☐
movement ☐	motionless ☐
speed ☐	rapid ☐

16

| break ☐ |
| relax ☐ |
| shiver ☐ |
| crack ☐ |
| interval ☐ |

17

| solid ☐ |
| stable ☐ |
| firm ☐ |
| organisation ☐ |
| determined ☐ |

18

| hole ☐ |
| crack ☐ |
| gap ☐ |
| rest ☐ |
| show ☐ |

19

| variety ☐ |
| style ☐ |
| kind ☐ |
| gentle ☐ |
| generous ☐ |

20

| ride ☐ |
| saddle ☐ |
| mount ☐ |
| astride ☐ |
| surge ☐ |

21

| C ☐ |
| H ☐ |
| A ☐ |
| R ☐ |

22

| T ☐ |
| R ☐ |
| A ☐ |
| I ☐ |
| N ☐ |

23

| B ☐ |
| R ☐ |
| A ☐ |
| C ☐ |
| E ☐ |

24

| R ☐ |
| O ☐ |
| A ☐ |
| M ☐ |

25

| M ☐ |
| I ☐ |
| S ☐ |
| E ☐ |
| R ☐ |
| Y ☐ |

Short Revision Paper 10

In the questions below, choose two words – one from each bracket – that will together make one correctly spelt word, without changing the order of the letters. The word from the bracket on the left always comes first. Mark the correct two words on the answer sheet.

1. (HIGH BE BELL)   (HIVE TOP LOW)

2. (HIDE STOP OVER)   (COVER TURN WALK)

3. (DOG TRUMP CAR)   (TRACK BIKE PET)

4. (LIGHT NIGHT OUT)   (FALL DAY SUN)

5. (NECK TIE KNOT)   (ROUND BOW LACE)

In the questions below, the words are in pairs. Mark on your answer sheet the word that completes the last pair in the same way as other pairs in each question. The word you make must be a real word.

6. PAINT   PANT : BOUND   BOND : FIEND   _____

7. NAIL   JAIL : RUMP   JUMP : PETTY   _____

8. SPIN   WIN : MOON   WON : AFAR   _____

9. CREATURE CAT : DREAMY DAM : RESIDE   _____

10. STORE   ROSE : PLACE · CAPE : CRIME   _____

In the questions below, mark on your answer sheet the two words – one from each bracket – that are closest in meaning.

11. (plead expand shrink)   (diminish guilty large)

12. (happy elation jealous)   (despair envious sad)

13. (boast strange injure)   (known handicap brag)

14. (devise courage mix)   (bravery part separate)

15. (still movement speed)   (reduce motionless rapid)

In the following questions, there are two pairs of words in brackets and a list of words underneath. Find the word from the list that goes equally well with both pairs in the brackets. Mark the correct answer on the answer sheet.

16.　(snap　pause)　　　(shatter　rest)
　　　break　relax　shiver　crack　interval

17.　(hard　rigid)　　　(company　business)
　　　solid　stable　firm　organisation　determined

18.　(opening　space)　(interval　pause)
　　　hole　crack　gap　rest　show

19.　(sort　type)　　　(helpful　affectionate)
　　　variety　style　kind　gentle　generous

20.　(ascend　climb)　(horse　pony)
　　　ride　saddle　mount　astride　surge

In the following questions, move one letter from the first word and place it into the second word to make two new words. Apart from this, the letters must not be rearranged. Mark the correct letter on the answer sheet.

21.　CHAR　　　AT

22.　TRAIN　　SAG

23.　BRACE　　EAT

24.　ROAM　　MAT

25.　MISERY　　OUR

Anthem Short Revision Papers
11+ and 12+ Verbal Reasoning Book 1
Answer Sheet 11

Please select your answers by filling in the correct boxes.

Name:

1

TRY	☐	PAST	☐
GOAL	☐	ATTEMPT	☐
ATTACK	☐	HARD	☐

2

PATH	☐	CRAWL	☐
SWIM	☐	STROLL	☐
WALK	☐	WATER	☐

3

SING	☐	MUSIC	☐
SCHOOL	☐	ASSEMBLE	☐
MEET	☐	LESSON	☐

4

ARRIVE	☐	RETAIN	☐
KEEP	☐	DEPART	☐
STAY	☐	CASTLE	☐

5

SMILING	☐	UNCERTAIN	☐
HAPPY	☐	BUSY	☐
DOUBTFUL	☐	FACE	☐

6

RIM	☐
SAD	☐
FIN	☐
ACT	☐
ANT	☐

7

RIM	☐
DIN	☐
AND	☐
SIN	☐
ASK	☐

8

RAG	☐
NOT	☐
SUM	☐
RIM	☐
RUM	☐

9

APE	☐
SAY	☐
LIP	☐
LAP	☐
TIP	☐

10

BEG	☐
LAY	☐
ATE	☐
RUG	☐
SAD	☐

11

five	☐	hundred	☐
ten	☐	thousand	☐
twenty	☐	year	☐

12

thin	☐	crowd	☐
weight	☐	small	☐
turkey	☐	cow	☐

13

house	☐	demolish	☐
construct	☐	bomb	☐
architect	☐	break	☐

14

side	☐	top	☐
front	☐	below	☐
above	☐	beneath	☐

15

note	☐	cover	☐
composer	☐	word	☐
instrument	☐	excitement	☐

16

23	☐
45	☐
19	☐
47	☐
28	☐

17

44	☐
14	☐
6	☐
12	☐
27	☐

18

3	☐
11	☐
13	☐
18	☐
21	☐

19

32	☐
24	☐
44	☐
56	☐
60	☐

20

8	☐
16	☐
4	☐
10	☐
14	☐

21

C	☐
O	☐
V	☐
E	☐
R	☐

22

C	☐
R	☐
A	☐
S	☐
H	☐

23

I	☐
E	☐
R	☐
C	☐
E	☐

24

H	☐
E	☐
A	☐
R	☐
T	☐

25

P	☐
L	☐
A	☐
N	☐
T	☐

Short Revision Paper 11

In the questions below, mark on your answer sheet the two words – one from each bracket – that are closest in meaning.

1. (TRY GOAL ATTACK)   (PAST ATTEMPT HARD)

2. (PATH SWIM WALK)   (CRAWL STROLL WATER)

3. (SING SCHOOL MEET)   (MUSIC ASSEMBLE LESSON)

4. (ARRIVE KEEP STAY)   (RETAIN DEPART CASTLE)

5. (SMILING HAPPY DOUBTFUL)   (UNCERTAIN BUSY FACE)

In each of the sentences below, three letters have been taken out of the word in capitals. These three letters, which make a proper word, will then make a correctly spelt word when inserted into the word in capitals. The completed sentence must make sense. Mark the word on your answer sheet.

6.   The FORY made parts for cars.

7.   The silver cup had two HLES.

8.   The DMER kept up a steady beat.

9.   The hairdresser regularly sharpened her CPERS.

10. The PFUL puppy ripped the carpet.

In the following questions select two words, one from each bracket, which complete the sentence in the best way. Mark the correct two words on the answer sheet.

11. Decade is to (five, ten, twenty) as century is to (hundred, thousand, year).

12. Plump is to (thin, weight, turkey) as big is to (crowd, small, cow).

13. Build is to (house, construct, architect) as destroy is to (demolish, bomb, break).

14. Back is to (side, front, above) as bottom is to (top, below, beneath).

15. Music is to (note, composer, instrument) as story is to (cover, word, excitement).

In the questions below, the numbers in each group are related in the same way. Find the number missing from the third group, and mark it on your answer sheet.

16.   5 (32) 6   8 (34) 4   9 ( ) 5

17.   10 (2) 6   24 (12) 10   34 ( ) 20

18.   20 (40) 10   15 (25) 5   8 ( ) 5

19.   3 (35) 4   6 (40) 2   8 ( ) 4

20.   15 (3) 6   40 (24) 8   12 ( ) 4

In the following questions, move one letter from the first word, and insert it into the second word to make two new words. Apart from this, the letters must not be rearranged. Mark the correct letter on the answer sheet.

21.   COVER   COOK

22.   CRASH   CHAT

23.   PIERCE   DIVE

24.   HEART   HASH

25.   PLANT   READ

Anthem Short Revision Papers
11+ and 12+ Verbal Reasoning Book 1
Answer Sheet 12

Please select your answers by filling in the correct boxes.

Name:

1
- KHET ☐
- KHES ☐
- KHEY ☐
- KGET ☐
- KIES ☐

2
- ITGF ☐
- ITLF ☐
- ITKJ ☐
- ITKF ☐
- ITKG ☐

3
- BPSQKFC ☐
- BPRQKFC ☐
- BPTQKFC ☐
- BOTLKFC ☐
- BLTLKFC ☐

4
- TKJT ☐
- TKJS ☐
- TKLS ☐
- TKJR ☐
- TKLR ☐

5
- NYWELQ ☐
- NYWEMQ ☐
- NYXEJQ ☐
- NYVXYT ☐
- NYWEJQ ☐

6
- 12 ☐
- 13 ☐
- 14 ☐
- 15 ☐
- 16 ☐

7
- 9 ☐
- 10 ☐
- 11 ☐
- 12 ☐
- 13 ☐

8
- 50 ☐
- 52 ☐
- 53 ☐
- 54 ☐
- 55 ☐

9
- 12 ☐
- 14 ☐
- 16 ☐
- 18 ☐
- 20 ☐

10
- 31 ☐
- 32 ☐
- 33 ☐
- 35 ☐
- 36 ☐

11
- ART ☐
- NOW ☐
- AIR ☐
- GAS ☐
- HERE ☐
- BRAKE ☐

12
- IN ☐
- OF ☐
- AN ☐
- CERTAIN ☐
- LESS ☐
- SURE ☐

13
- FOR ☐
- IN ☐
- WHEN ☐
- NONE ☐
- COME ☐
- SOME ☐

14
- PACK ☐
- HORSE ☐
- LOAD ☐
- TIME ☐
- AGE ☐
- PAST ☐

15
- PASS ☐
- STOP ☐
- GO ☐
- AIR ☐
- PORT ☐
- DOCK ☐

16
- shop only ☐
- only opened ☐
- opened on ☐
- on certain ☐
- certain days ☐

17
- small child ☐
- child could ☐
- reach inside ☐
- inside the ☐
- the cabinet ☐

18
- Place the ☐
- the meat ☐
- meat in ☐
- the hot ☐
- hot oven ☐

19
- Best not ☐
- not to ☐
- to shave ☐
- shave in ☐
- in cold ☐

20
- Rowdy pupils ☐
- pupils always ☐
- alway smake ☐
- teachers hopping ☐
- hopping mad ☐

21
- A ☐
- B ☐
- C ☐
- D ☐

22
- A ☐
- B ☐
- C ☐
- D ☐

23
- A ☐
- B ☐
- C ☐
- D ☐

24
- A ☐
- B ☐
- C ☐
- D ☐

25
- A ☐
- B ☐
- C ☐
- D ☐

Short Revision Paper 12

In the following questions, a word is represented by a code. Put the second word into the same code, which is different for each question. The alphabet is provided to help you. Mark the correct code on the answer sheet.

A B C D E F G H I J K L M N O P Q R S T U V W X Y Z

1.   If TOWN is represented by SNVM what represents LIFT?

2.   If SONG is represented by UQPI what represents GRID?

3.   If CROWDS is represented by BSNXCT what represents COUPLED?

4.   If CART is represented by DCUX what represents SIGN?

5.   If FONDUE is represented by HMPBWC what represents LAUGHS?

In the following questions, find the number that completes each series in the most sensible way. Mark it down on the answer sheet.

6.   1   2   4   7   11   —————————

7.   2   4   5   7   8   10   —————————

8.   8   11   17   26   38   —————————

9.   4   2   7   5   11   9   16   —————————

10.   2   3   5   9   17   —————————

In the following questions, choose two words – one from each bracket – that will together make one correctly spelt word, without changing the order of the letters. The word from the bracket on the left always comes first. Mark the correct pair of words on the answer sheet.

11.   (ART   NOW   AIR)   (GAS   HERE   BRAKE)

12.   (IN   OF   AN)   (CERTAIN   LESS   SURE)

13.   (FOR   IN   WHEN)   (NONE   COME   SOME)

14.   (PACK   HORSE   LOAD)   (TIME   AGE   PAST)

15.   (PASS   STOP   GO)   (AIR   PORT   DOCK)

In each of the following questions, there is a word hidden at the end of one word and the beginning of the next. Find the pair that contains the hidden word. Mark the correct pair of words on the answer sheet.

16.   The shop only opened on certain days.

17.   The small child could not reach inside the cabinet.

18.   Place the meat in the hot oven.

19.   Best not to shave in cold water.

20.   Rowdy pupils always make teachers hopping mad.

In the following questions, the letters stand for numbers. Work out the answers to the sums, and mark them on your answer sheet, giving your answer as a letter.

$A = 4$ $B = 8$ $C = 20$ $D = 12$

21. $A + B$

22. $C - D$

23. $A - D + C$

24. $2B + A$

25. $D + C \div B$

Anthem Short Revision Papers
11+ and 12+ Verbal Reasoning Book 1
Answer Sheet 13

Please select your answers by filling in the correct boxes.

Name:

1
- alone ☐
- prison ☐
- solitary ☐
- single ☐
- punishment ☐

2
- brave ☐
- medal ☐
- courageous ☐
- heroic ☐
- fearful ☐

3
- chaos ☐
- noisy ☐
- order ☐
- jumble ☐
- mess ☐

4
- pleasure ☐
- delight ☐
- circus ☐
- clown ☐
- enjoyment ☐

5
- dwell ☐
- house ☐
- abode ☐
- inhabit ☐
- live ☐

6
- DIP ☐
- WIN ☐
- COW ☐
- WAR ☐
- WAS ☐

7
- MEN ☐
- ROW ☐
- AND ☐
- PIN ☐
- RAW ☐

8
- DIM ☐
- SIP ☐
- ASK ☐
- ARK ☐
- CAR ☐

9
- ASK ☐
- RAW ☐
- CAN ☐
- DID ☐
- MAN ☐

10
- LOW ☐
- RAN ☐
- DIG ☐
- LIT ☐
- COG ☐

11
- 62 ☐
- 63 ☐
- 64 ☐
- 65 ☐
- 66 ☐

12
- 18 ☐
- 20 ☐
- 22 ☐
- 25 ☐
- 27 ☐

13
- 96 ☐
- 144 ☐
- 192 ☐
- 240 ☐
- 288 ☐

14
- 22 ☐
- 23 ☐
- 25 ☐
- 26 ☐
- 27 ☐

15
- 27 ☐
- 28 ☐
- 29 ☐
- 30 ☐
- 31 ☐

16
- CARD ☐
- PAL ☐
- SUPER ☐
- FRIEND ☐
- PETROL ☐
- ACE ☐

17
- EGG ☐
- HID ☐
- FOUR ☐
- YOLK ☐
- DEN ☐
- MOST ☐

18
- PEAS ☐
- PLEASE ☐
- GROUND ☐
- SURE ☐
- ARE ☐
- ANT ☐

19
- TERMINUS ☐
- GROUND ☐
- ROT ☐
- ATE ☐
- BUS ☐
- PLAY ☐

20
- UNDER ☐
- GRIM ☐
- NEVER ☐
- SURFACE ☐
- ACE ☐
- THE ☐

21
- T ☐
- H ☐
- I ☐
- N ☐

22
- T ☐
- H ☐
- I ☐
- N ☐
- K ☐

23
- S ☐
- W ☐
- O ☐
- R ☐
- D ☐

24
- R ☐
- I ☐
- N ☐
- K ☐

25
- C ☐
- R ☐
- O ☐
- W ☐

Short Revision Paper 13

In the following questions, two words do not belong with the other three. Mark the two odd ones out on your answer sheet.

1. alone   prison   solitary   single   punishment

2. brave   medal   courageous   heroic   fearful

3. chaos   noisy   order   jumble   mess

4. pleasure   delight   circus   clown   enjoyment

5. dwell   house   abode   inhabit   live

In each of the sentences below, three letters have been taken out of the word in capitals. These three letters, which make a proper word, will then make a correctly spelt word when inserted into the word in capitals. The completed sentence must make sense. Mark the word on your answer sheet.

6. The ARD ran away from the danger.

7. The stadium was CDED with spectators.

8. The sky DENED as the sun set over the horizon.

9. The highwayman DEDED all money and jewellery.

10. The FERS added brightness to the room.

In the following questions, find the number that completes each series in the most sensible way. Mark the correct number on the answer sheet.

11. 6   13   21   30   40   51   _____

12. 6   6   8   8   11   10   15   12   _____

13. 2   4   12   48   _____

14. 3   4   7   8   12   12   18   16   _____

15. 5   7   11   9   17   11   23   13   _____

In the following questions, choose two words – one from each bracket – that will together make one correctly spelt word, without changing the order of the letters. The word from the bracket on the left always comes first. Mark the correct words on the answer sheet.

16.   (CARD   PAL   SUPER)   (FRIEND   PETROL   ACE)

17.   (EGG   HID   FOUR)   (YOLK   DEN   MOST)

18.   (PEAS   PLEASE   GROUND)   (SURE   ARE   ANT)

19.   (TERMINUS   GROUND   ROT)   (ATE   BUS   PLAY)

20.   (UNDER   GRIM   NEVER)   (SURFACE   ACE   THE)

In the following questions, one letter can be moved from the first word to the second word to make two new words. Apart from this, the letters must not be rearranged, and both new words must make sense. Mark the correct letter on the answer sheet.

21.   THIN   SIP

22.   THINK   NOW

23.   SWORD   FEAT

24.   RINK   EAR

25.   CROW   ONE

Anthem Short Revision Papers
11+ and 12+ Verbal Reasoning Book 1
Answer Sheet 14

Please select your answers by filling in the correct boxes.

Name:

1
- guarantee ☐
- receive ☐
- welcome ☐
- agree ☐
- pledge ☐

2
- segregate ☐
- escorted ☐
- divided ☐
- lonely ☐
- alone ☐

3
- awkward ☐
- difficult ☐
- careless ☐
- ungainly ☐
- thoughtless ☐

4
- back ☐
- reinforce ☐
- withdraw ☐
- defend ☐
- encourage ☐

5
- blow ☐
- tragedy ☐
- thump ☐
- smack ☐
- calamity ☐

6
- DROOP ☐
- DROWN ☐
- DRUGS ☐
- DROPS ☐
- DRIPS ☐

7
- PATE ☐
- TAPE ☐
- TRAP ☐
- PEAT ☐
- PART ☐

8
- XTTBTW ☐
- XTSATW ☐
- XTTART ☐
- XTUAWT ☐
- XTTAWT ☐

9
- EBZBT ☐
- EBZCS ☐
- EBCZT ☐
- EBYCT ☐
- EBWCT ☐

10
- XDYQD ☐
- XDZQD ☐
- XDYSD ☐
- XDXQD ☐
- XDRQZ ☐

11
- I ☐
- J ☐
- K ☐
- L ☐
- M ☐

12
- M ☐
- N ☐
- O ☐
- P ☐
- Q ☐

13
- D ☐
- E ☐
- F ☐
- G ☐
- H ☐

14
- AP ☐
- AO ☐
- BO ☐
- BP ☐
- CP ☐

15
- NH ☐
- MG ☐
- OH ☐
- MH ☐
- PG ☐

16
- 35 ☐
- 40 ☐
- 45 ☐
- 50 ☐
- 60 ☐

17
- 17 ☐
- 18 ☐
- 19 ☐
- 20 ☐
- 21 ☐

18
- 40 ☐
- 32 ☐
- 20 ☐
- 6 ☐
- 4 ☐

19
- 4 ☐
- 8 ☐
- 18 ☐
- 32 ☐
- 56 ☐

20
- 21 ☐
- 22 ☐
- 20 ☐
- 24 ☐
- 25 ☐

21
- TAB ☐
- BAT ☐
- SAT ☐
- ASS ☐

22
- CAN ☐
- CAT ☐
- ANT ☐
- TAN ☐

23
- STAB ☐
- TABS ☐
- TAME ☐
- BATS ☐

24
- BONE ☐
- DONE ☐
- NOON ☐
- ONCE ☐

25
- LUMP ☐
- PULP ☐
- SLUM ☐
- SUMP ☐

Short Revision Paper 14

In the following questions, there are two pairs of words in brackets and a list of words underneath. Find the word from the list that goes equally well with both pairs in the brackets. Mark the correct word on the answer sheet.

1. (accept acknowledge)   (consent promise)
    guarantee receive welcome   agree pledge

2. (separately unaccompanied)   (solitary isolated)
    segregate escorted divided lonely alone

3. (bulky clumsy)   (stubborn unhelpful)
    awkward difficult careless ungainly thoughtless

4. (revise retreat)   (help support)
    back reinforce withdraw defend encourage

5. (slap punch)   (disaster upset)
    blow tragedy thump smack calamity

In the following questions, a different code is used for each question. Work out the answers marking the correct answer on the answer sheet. An alphabet is provided to help you.

A B C D E F G H I J K L M N O P Q R S T U V W X Y Z

6. If ABCDE stands for CROWD and FCXYE stands for SOUND what does EBCDY stand for?

7. If ABCD stands for CART and XYZQ stands for HOPE what does ZQBD stand for?

8. If XYZT stands for BAND and PTAW stands for JOKE what stands for BOOKED?

9. If XYZT stands for GOAL and ABCDE stands for PRINT what stands for TRIAL?

10. If XYZQD stands for SCAMP and ABXD stands for GUST what stands for STAMP?

In the following questions, select the letter/s that best completes the series. The alphabet is provided to help you. Mark the correct letter or letters on the answer sheet.

A B C D E F G H I J K L M N O P Q R S T U V W X Y Z

11. C B E C G D I E ＿＿＿＿＿＿

12. B B D D F G H K J ＿＿＿＿＿＿

13. Z Y W T P K ＿＿＿＿＿＿

14. MZ PX SV VT YR ＿＿＿＿＿＿

15. CB EC GD IE KF ＿＿＿＿＿＿

In the following questions, the three numbers in each group are related in the same way. Find the number that completes the last group. Mark the correct answer on the answer sheet.

16. 6 (16) 10   7 (19) 12   15 ( ) 30

17. 10 (12) 7   18 (19) 10   22 ( ) 8

18. 24 (3) 8   40 (5) 8   48 ( ) 8

19. 60 (10) 12   48 (4) 24   80 ( ) 20

20. 6 (22) 5   4 (26) 9   7 ( ) 3

In each question below the words are in pairs. Complete the last pair in the same way as the first two. Mark the correct word on the answer sheet.

21. STUNT NUT   : STORE ROT   : STABS ＿＿＿＿＿＿

22. STAIN TAN   : TRAIN RAN   : SCANT ＿＿＿＿＿＿

23. MACE CAME   : MATE TAME : TABS ＿＿＿＿＿＿

24. BARE CARE   : SOOT TOOT : CONE ＿＿＿＿＿＿

25. SHOP HOPS   : SCAR CARS : PLUM ＿＿＿＿＿＿

Anthem Short Revision Papers
11+ and 12+ Verbal Reasoning Book 1
Answer Sheet 15

Please select your answers by filling in the correct boxes.

Name:

1
- dodge ☐
- attack ☐
- link ☐
- both ☐
- evade ☐

2
- intense ☐
- dazzling ☐
- glare ☐
- expression ☐
- glower ☐

3
- disaster ☐
- surprise ☐
- hit ☐
- knock ☐
- achievement ☐

4
- scale ☐
- clamber ☐
- enlarge ☐
- length ☐
- mount ☐

5
- outing ☐
- expedition ☐
- trip ☐
- collapse ☐
- pitch ☐

6
- H ☐
- T ☐
- G ☐
- E ☐
- B ☐

7
- T ☐
- R ☐
- P ☐
- S ☐
- D ☐

8
- E ☐
- S ☐
- T ☐
- N ☐
- B ☐

9
- P ☐
- L ☐
- R ☐
- T ☐
- S ☐

10
- E ☐
- S ☐
- L ☐
- B ☐
- H ☐

11
- OUST ☐
- SORT ☐
- ROUT ☐
- RUST ☐
- TOUR ☐

12
- OUST ☐
- SORT ☐
- ROUT ☐
- RUST ☐
- TOUR ☐

13
- OUST ☐
- SORT ☐
- ROUT ☐
- RUST ☐
- TOUR ☐

14
- OUST ☐
- SORT ☐
- ROUT ☐
- RUST ☐
- TOUR ☐

15
- OUST ☐
- SORT ☐
- ROUT ☐
- RUST ☐
- TOUR ☐

16
- book ☐
- write ☐
- print ☐
- music ☐
- orchestra ☐
- beat ☐

17
- four ☐
- cuboid ☐
- maths ☐
- degree ☐
- three ☐
- geometry ☐

18
- ruler ☐
- line ☐
- centimetre ☐
- calendar ☐
- date ☐
- decade ☐

19
- rein ☐
- wet ☐
- weather ☐
- place ☐
- location ☐
- hear ☐

20
- bad ☐
- wicked ☐
- giant ☐
- gigantic ☐
- dwarf ☐
- small ☐

21
- RT ☐
- RS ☐
- QS ☐
- RU ☐
- ST ☐

22
- KL ☐
- KM ☐
- KP ☐
- NP ☐
- PR ☐

23
- PH ☐
- QH ☐
- KM ☐
- KN ☐
- KH ☐

24
- YX ☐
- YZ ☐
- YY ☐
- WX ☐
- VX ☐

25
- WB ☐
- WD ☐
- WC ☐
- ZC ☐
- XC ☐

Short Revision Paper 15

In the following questions, there are two pairs of words in brackets and a list of words underneath. Find the word from the list that goes equally well with both pairs in the brackets. Mark the correct word on the answer sheet.

1. (fasten   secure)   (escape   flee)
    dodge   attack   bolt   both   evade

2. (brightness   brilliance)   (frown   scowl)
    intense   dazzling   glare   expression   glower

3. (blow   knock)   (success   triumph)
    disaster   surprise   hit   knock   achievement

4. (climb   ascend)   (grow   increase)
    scale   clamber   enlarge   length   mount

5. (excursion   visit)   (stagger   tumble)
    outing   expedition   trip   collapse   pitch

In each of the questions below, find one letter that will both complete the word in front of the brackets and begin the word after the brackets. The same letter must complete both sets of words. Mark it down on the answer sheet.

6.   SIN   ( )   ATE   :   THIN   ( )   ONE

7.   KIN   ( )   ARK   :   TREN   ( )   ANCE

8.   COM   ( )   ONE   :   BUL   ( )   EAR

9.   SEA   ( )   IVER   :   PEA   ( )   IMP

10. LIM   ( )   AND   :   HER   ( )   ONE

In the following questions, OUST, SORT, ROUT, RUST and TOUR are written in code. The same code has been used for all of the words. Out of these five words, which is the correct word for each question? Mark it down on the answer sheet.

11.   5 1 2 4

12.   4 1 2 5

13.   3 1 5 4

14.   5 2 3 4

15.   1 2 3 4

In the following questions, find the two words – one from each group – that will complete the sentence in the best way.

16.   Author is to (book, write, print) as composer is to (music, orchestra, beat).

17.   Rectangle is to (four, cuboid, maths) as triangle is to (degree, three, geometry).

18.   Millimetre is to (ruler, line, centimetre) as year is to (calendar, date, decade).

19.   Rain is to (rein, wet, weather) as here is to (place, location, hear).

20.   Evil is to (bad, wicket, giant) as huge is to (gigantic, dwarf, small).

In the following questions, select the letters that complete the sentences in the best way. The alphabet is provided to help you. Mark the correct letters on the answer sheet.

A B C D E F G H I J K L M N O P Q R S T U V W X Y Z

21.   FH is to HJ as PR is to ――――――――

22.   JK is to HM as MN is to ――――――――

23.   NP is to QN as HJ is to ――――――――

24.   DF is to IJ as TV is to ――――――――

25.   WX is to UA as YZ is to ――――――――

Anthem Short Revision Papers
11+ and 12+ Verbal Reasoning Book 1
Answer Sheet 16

Please select your answers by filling in the correct boxes.

Name:

1
- L ☐
- I ☐
- D ☐
- E ☐

2
- R ☐
- A ☐
- F ☐
- T ☐

3
- R ☐
- O ☐
- A ☐
- D ☐

4
- C ☐
- A ☐
- R ☐
- E ☐

5
- H ☐
- E ☐
- A ☐
- T ☐

6
- 38 ☐
- 39 ☐
- 40 ☐
- 41 ☐
- 42 ☐

7
- 68 ☐
- 69 ☐
- 70 ☐
- 71 ☐
- 72 ☐

8
- 6 ☐
- 7 ☐
- 8 ☐
- 9 ☐
- 10 ☐

9
- 10 ☐
- 11 ☐
- 12 ☐
- 13 ☐
- 14 ☐

10
- 14 ☐
- 15 ☐
- 16 ☐
- 17 ☐
- 18 ☐

11
- J ☐
- K ☐
- L ☐
- M ☐
- N ☐

12
- S ☐
- T ☐
- U ☐
- V ☐
- W ☐

13
- M ☐
- N ☐
- O ☐
- P ☐
- Q ☐

14
- MK ☐
- ML ☐
- MM ☐
- LK ☐
- NK ☐

15
- JD ☐
- JF ☐
- JE ☐
- KE ☐
- IE ☐

16
- mouth ☐
- claw ☐
- tooth ☐
- dentist ☐
- person ☐
- eat ☐

17
- colour ☐
- channel ☐
- sight ☐
- music ☐
- volume ☐
- sound ☐

18
- tea ☐
- sweet ☐
- white ☐
- dessert ☐
- sour ☐
- red ☐

19
- golf ☐
- whole ☐
- drill ☐
- meat ☐
- meal ☐
- stake ☐

20
- drink ☐
- liquid ☐
- thirst ☐
- gate ☐
- rod ☐
- solid ☐

21
- The teacher ☐
- teacher or ☐
- the dinner ☐
- look after ☐
- after you ☐

22
- The advert ☐
- advert proved ☐
- proved to ☐
- to be ☐
- very successful ☐

23
- Some alloys ☐
- alloys are ☐
- are weaker ☐
- weaker than ☐
- than others ☐

24
- A banana ☐
- banana and ☐
- and orange ☐
- are good ☐
- good breakfast ☐

25
- It was ☐
- was his ☐
- his luck ☐
- idea to ☐
- to sing ☐

Short Revision Paper 16

In the following questions, one letter can be moved from the first word to the second word to make two new words. Apart from this, the letters must not be rearranged, and both new words must make sense. Mark the correct letter on the answer sheet.

1. SLIDE   POD

2. RAFT   RULE

3. ROAD   PET

4. CARE   CAN

5. HEAT   CAT

In the following questions, complete the series in the same pattern. Mark the correct number on the answer sheet.

6.   1   5   10   16   23   31   _____

7.   90   88   85   81   76   _____

8.   2   3   4   4   6   5   _____

9.   5   6   7   7   9   8   _____

10.   6   8·5   11   13·5   _____

In the following questions, complete the series in the best way. The alphabet is provided to help you. Mark the correct letter/s on the answer sheet.

A B C D E F G H I J K L M N O P Q R S T U V W X Y Z

11.   B   D   F   H   J   _____

12.   A   C   F   J   O   _____

13.   Z   X   V   T   R   _____

14.   AC   DE   GG   JI   _____

15.   TU   RW   PY   NA   LC   _____

In the following questions, select the two words – one from each bracket – that complete the sentence in the best way.

16.   Teeth is to (mouth, claw, tooth) as people is to (dentist, person, eat).

17.   Television is to (colour, channel, sight) as radio is to (music, volume, sound).

18.   Sugar is to (tea, sweet, white) as lemon is to (dessert, sour, red).

19.   Hole is to (golf, whole, drill) as steak is to (meat, meal, stake).

20.   Water is to (drink, liquid, thirst) as iron is to (gate, rod, solid).

In the sentences below, a word of four letters is hidden at the end of one word and the beginning of the next. Mark the pair of words that contain the hidden word on your answer sheet.

21.   The teacher or the dinner lady will look after you.

22.   The advert proved to be successful.

23.   Some alloys are weaker than others.

24.   A banana and an orange are good for breakfast.

25.   It was his luck to sing.

Anthem Short Revision Papers
11+ and 12+ Verbal Reasoning Book 1
Answer Sheet 17

Please select your answers by filling in the correct boxes.

Name:

1
- murky ☐
- black ☐
- gloom ☐
- grief ☐
- despair ☐

2
- catch ☐
- problems ☐
- handle ☐
- grip ☐
- hook ☐

3
- frozen ☐
- cool ☐
- casual ☐
- smooth ☐
- mild ☐

4
- congestion ☐
- obstruct ☐
- jam ☐
- problem ☐
- squeeze ☐

5
- rise ☐
- weigh ☐
- measurement ☐
- scale ☐
- activity ☐

6

PORT ☐	PUT ☐
CORD ☐	HEAD ☐
NO ☐	ABLE ☐

7

RAN ☐	LESS ☐
SET ☐	SACK ☐
BE ☐	PAIN ☐

8

BUSH ☐	BY ☐
CART ☐	IN ☐
STEP ☐	ON ☐

9

SAP ☐	ON ☐
IT ☐	LANE ☐
IN ☐	LET ☐

10

CAN ☐	HIM ☐
CUP ☐	NON ☐
CAT ☐	HER ☐

11
- SEA ☐
- DIE ☐
- SAD ☐
- SEE ☐
- AID ☐

12
- LACK ☐
- TOIL ☐
- COIL ☐
- COOK ☐
- TOOK ☐

13
- NOON ☐
- HORN ☐
- ZOOM ☐
- RUIN ☐
- ROOM ☐

14
- SIT ☐
- LIT ☐
- BIT ☐
- KIT ☐
- FIT ☐

15
- CLAP ☐
- SLAP ☐
- LAPS ☐
- PALS ☐
- ALPS ☐

16
- MEAN ☐
- MEAL ☐
- MEAT ☐
- MEET ☐
- MATE ☐

17
- PALE ☐
- PAST ☐
- PASS ☐
- PACE ☐
- PAID ☐

18
- PART ☐
- PORT ☐
- POOR ☐
- POET ☐
- PLAN ☐

19
- CART ☐
- CARE ☐
- CALM ☐
- CALF ☐
- CARP ☐

20
- SOAP ☐
- SOUP ☐
- SOAK ☐
- SORE ☐
- SOLD ☐

21
- 4 ☐
- 20 ☐
- 30 ☐
- 36 ☐
- 40 ☐

22
- 17 ☐
- 1 ☐
- 72 ☐
- 81 ☐
- 63 ☐

23
- 5 ☐
- 6 ☐
- 7 ☐
- 8 ☐
- 9 ☐

24
- 24 ☐
- 6 ☐
- 36 ☐
- 30 ☐
- 44 ☐

25
- 35 ☐
- 45 ☐
- 50 ☐
- 55 ☐
- 56 ☐

Short Revision Paper 17

In the following questions, there are two pairs of words in brackets and a list of words underneath. Find the word from the list that goes equally well with both pairs in the brackets. Mark the correct word on the answer sheet.

1. (darkness shadow)   (misery sadness)
    murky black gloom grief despair

2. (snag difficulty)   (latch clasp)
    catch problems handle grip hook

3. (chilled ice)   (calm unruffled)
    frozen cool casual smooth mild

4. (crush bottleneck)   (difficulty plight)
    congestion obstruct jam problem squeeze

5. (climb ascend)   (balance music)
    rise weigh measurement scale activity

In the questions below, select two words – one from each set – that together make a correctly spelt word, without changing the order of the letters. The word on the left always comes first. Mark the correct words on the answer sheet.

6. (PORT CORD NO)   (PUT HEAD ABLE)

7. (RAN SET BE)   (LESS SACK PAIN)

8. (BUSH CART STEP)   (BY IN ON)

9. (SAP IT IN)   (ON LANE LET)

10. (CAN CUP CAT)   (HIM NON HER)

In the following questions, the words are in pairs. Complete the last pair in the same way as the first two. Mark the correct word on the answer sheet.

11. BARREN BAN   :   EARNEST   EAT   :   DISEASE   _____

12. POCKET POET : DISGRACE DICE : COCKTAIL _____

13. DIRECT DIRT : MANICURE MANE : HORIZON _____

14. PILL   LIP   : WALL   LAW   : TILL   _____

15. SCORE CORE : BOAST   BOAT : CLASP   _____

In the following questions, a different code is used for each question. Work out the answers marking the correct answer on the answer sheet. An alphabet is provided to help you.

A B C D E F G H I J K L M N O P Q R S T U V W X Y Z

16.   If LIFE is represented by MJGF what does NFBM represent?

17.   If HOPE is represented by IQSI what does QCVX represent?

18.   If PASS is represented by QZTR what does QNSS represent?

19.   If YOUR is represented by YNSO what does CZPB represent?

20.   If ROPE is represented by RPPF what does SPAL represent?

The following groups of numbers are related in the same way. Complete the third group in the series in the same way as the first two. Mark the correct number on the answer sheet.

21.   5 (16) 11   11 (20) 9   17 ( ) 13

22.   3 (15) 5   7 (28) 4   9 ( ) 8

23.   20 (4) 5   36 (9) 4   35 ( ) 7

24.   7 (20) 6   15 (33) 3   12 ( ) 6

25.   4 (30) 5   6 (40) 5   9 ( ) 5

Anthem Short Revision Papers
11+ and 12+ Verbal Reasoning Book 1
Answer Sheet 18

Please select your answers by filling in the correct boxes.

Name:

1
- HUT ☐
- HAT ☐
- SAP ☐
- HIT ☐
- SAT ☐

2
- PAY ☐
- DID ☐
- OIL ☐
- SAD ☐
- MAD ☐

3
- SAD ☐
- RUB ☐
- RUM ☐
- CAN ☐
- RAN ☐

4
- TIN ☐
- TAN ☐
- TRY ☐
- RIM ☐
- SAG ☐

5
- PAT ☐
- PIN ☐
- CAT ☐
- CUP ☐
- CAP ☐

6
- football ☐
- attendance ☐
- roar ☐
- stadium ☐
- play ☐
- silence ☐

7
- bike ☐
- speed ☐
- health ☐
- plane ☐
- height ☐
- journey ☐

8
- glass ☐
- open ☐
- reflection ☐
- wood ☐
- close ☐
- lock ☐

9
- injury ☐
- soar ☐
- pain ☐
- park ☐
- stag ☐
- dear ☐

10
- rare ☐
- often ☐
- punctual ☐
- surprise ☐
- present ☐
- secret ☐

11
- 10 ☐
- 11 ☐
- 12 ☐
- 13 ☐
- 14 ☐

12
- 32 ☐
- 37 ☐
- 63 ☐
- 73 ☐
- 84 ☐

13
- 32 ☐
- 33 ☐
- 34 ☐
- 35 ☐
- 36 ☐

14
- 64 ☐
- 122 ☐
- 126 ☐
- 252 ☐
- 256 ☐

15
- 2 ☐
- 3 ☐
- 4 ☐
- 5 ☐
- 6 ☐

16
- F ☐
- E ☐
- U ☐
- D ☐

17
- P ☐
- A ☐
- T ☐
- C ☐
- H ☐

18
- S ☐
- P ☐
- L ☐
- I ☐
- T ☐

19
- Q ☐
- U ☐
- I ☐
- E ☐
- T ☐

20
- G ☐
- R ☐
- O ☐
- W ☐
- S ☐

21
- display ☐
- sale ☐
- customer ☐
- shop ☐
- reveal ☐
- window ☐

22
- hoard ☐
- bank ☐
- famine ☐
- money ☐
- food ☐
- save ☐

23
- war ☐
- conquest ☐
- oppose ☐
- resist ☐
- enemy ☐
- military ☐

24
- peace ☐
- command ☐
- officer ☐
- army ☐
- soldier ☐
- instruction ☐

25
- register ☐
- maths ☐
- presence ☐
- attendance ☐
- fractions ☐
- school ☐

Short Revision Paper 18

In each of the sentences below, three letters have been taken out of the word in capitals. These three letters, which make a proper word, will then make a correctly spelt word when inserted into the word in capitals. The completed sentence must make sense. Mark the word on your answer sheet.

1. The glass STERED when it hit the ground.

2. Children who are SPT cry when they don't get their own way.

3. The waves CBLED the base of the cliff.

4. The chef was proud of his delicious PAS.

5. The dropped notes STERED in the wind.

In the questions below, choose one word from each bracket that will complete the sentence in the best way. Mark the correct words on the answer sheet.

6. Spectator is to (football, attendance, roar) as audience is to (stadium, play, silence).

7. Cycle is to (bike, speed, health) as fly is to (plane, height, journey).

8. Window is to (glass, open, reflection) as door is to (wood, close, lock).

9. Sore is to (injury, soar, pain) as deer is to (park, stag, dear).

10. Frequent is to (rare, often, punctual) as amaze is to (surprise, present, secret).

In each of the following questions, find the number that completes the series in the best way. Mark the correct number on the answer sheet.

11. 4 4 6 7 8 10 10 ⎯⎯⎯⎯⎯⎯

12. 1 3 7 15 31 ⎯⎯⎯⎯⎯⎯

13. 53 56 47 49 41 42 35 ⎯⎯⎯⎯⎯⎯

14. 15 30 31 62 63 ⎯⎯⎯⎯⎯⎯

15. 9 8 7 6 5 4 3 ⎯⎯⎯⎯⎯⎯

In the following questions, move one letter from the first word into the second word to make two new words. Apart from this, the letters must not be rearranged. Mark the correct letter on the answer sheet.

16. FEUD   BOND

17. PATCH   RASH

18. SPLIT   PAY

19. QUIET   MET

20. GROW   ROUND

In the following questions, select two words – one from each bracket – that are closest in meaning. Mark the correct words on the answer sheet.

21. (display   sale   customer)   (shop   reveal   window)

22. (hoard   bank   famine)   (money   food   save)

23. (war   conquest   oppose)   (resist   enemy   military)

24. (peace   command   officer)   (army   soldier   instruction)

25. (register   maths   presence)   (attendance   fractions   school)

Anthem Short Revision Papers
11+ and 12+ Verbal Reasoning Book 1
Answer Sheet 19

Please select your answers by filling in the correct boxes.

Name:

1
calamity ☐	injury ☐
accident ☐	disaster ☐
crash ☐	flood ☐

2
rough ☐	sea ☐
shy ☐	windy ☐
calm ☐	peaceful ☐

3
science ☐	melt ☐
dissolve ☐	experiment ☐
ice ☐	lessson ☐

4
smile ☐	scowl ☐
humour ☐	temper ☐
frown ☐	comedian ☐

5
save ☐	spendthrift ☐
misery ☐	sadness ☐
enthusiasm ☐	rush ☐

6
| LN ☐ |
| NO ☐ |
| NP ☐ |
| LP ☐ |
| NM ☐ |

7
| T ☐ |
| U ☐ |
| V ☐ |
| W ☐ |
| X ☐ |

8
| H ☐ |
| I ☐ |
| J ☐ |
| K ☐ |
| L ☐ |

9
| W ☐ |
| X ☐ |
| Y ☐ |
| Z ☐ |
| A ☐ |

10
| QR ☐ |
| QS ☐ |
| QY ☐ |
| RY ☐ |
| PY ☐ |

11
| M ☐ |
| N ☐ |
| B ☐ |
| P ☐ |
| Q ☐ |

12
| M ☐ |
| N ☐ |
| B ☐ |
| P ☐ |
| Q ☐ |

13
| M ☐ |
| N ☐ |
| B ☐ |
| P ☐ |
| Q ☐ |

14
| M ☐ |
| N ☐ |
| B ☐ |
| P ☐ |
| Q ☐ |

15
| M ☐ |
| N ☐ |
| B ☐ |
| P ☐ |
| Q ☐ |

16
| SPIN ☐ |
| PAIN ☐ |
| PINS ☐ |
| SPAN ☐ |
| PANS ☐ |

17
| SPIN ☐ |
| PAIN ☐ |
| PINS ☐ |
| SPAN ☐ |
| PANS ☐ |

18
| SPIN ☐ |
| PAIN ☐ |
| PINS ☐ |
| SPAN ☐ |
| PANS ☐ |

19
| SPIN ☐ |
| PAIN ☐ |
| PINS ☐ |
| SPAN ☐ |
| PANS ☐ |

20
| SPIN ☐ |
| PAIN ☐ |
| PINS ☐ |
| SPAN ☐ |
| PANS ☐ |

21
| ARCH ☐ |
| HAIR ☐ |
| MAIN ☐ |
| CHIN ☐ |
| CHAR ☐ |

22
| ERA ☐ |
| ARE ☐ |
| RAN ☐ |
| CAR ☐ |
| CAN ☐ |

23
| REST ☐ |
| TEAR ☐ |
| BARE ☐ |
| WEAR ☐ |
| BEAR ☐ |

24
| FOIL ☐ |
| FOOL ☐ |
| FAIR ☐ |
| FLAT ☐ |
| FLIT ☐ |

25
| TALE ☐ |
| LATE ☐ |
| TEAR ☐ |
| LEVY ☐ |
| RAVE ☐ |

Short Revision Paper 19

In the following questions, select the two words – one from each bracket – that are closest in meaning. Mark the correct words on the answer sheet.

1. (calamity   accident   crash)   (injury   disaster   flood)

2. (rough   shy   calm)   (sea   windy   peaceful)

3. (science   dissolve   ice)   (melt   experiment   lesson)

4. (smile   humour   frown)   (scowl   temper   comedian)

5. (save   misery   enthusiasm)   (spendthrift   sadness   rush)

In the questions below, find the letter/s that best completes the series. The alphabet is provided to help you. Mark the correct answers on the answer sheet.

A B C D E F G H I J K L M N O P Q R S T U V W X Y Z

6.   BA   DC   FE   HG   JI   LK _____

7.   B   F   J   N   R _____

8.   A   Y   C   W   E   U   G   S _____

9.   S   Q   N   J   E _____

10. BN   EK   HH   KE   NB _____

In the following questions, letters stand for numbers. Work out the answers to the sums, and mark them on your answer sheet, giving your answer as a letter.

$M = 6$ $N = 2$ $B = 4$ $P = 5$ $Q = 1$

11. $N + P - Q$

12. $M - P + Q$

13. $M + N - P + N$

14. $(M + B) \div P$

15. $Q (N + B)$

The following five words, SPIN, PAIN, PINS, SPAN and PANS are written in code. The same code is used throughout this section. Match each question with the correct word. Mark it down on the answer sheet.

16. 1 3 4 5

17. 1 3 6 4

18. 5 1 6 4

19. 5 1 3 4

20. 1 6 4 5

In the following questions there should be two groups of three words. The three on the right go together in the same way as the three on the left. Find the missing word, and mark it down on the answer sheet.

21. SPIN   (SPAN)   LEAN   :   CHUM (   )   RAIN

22. FEET   (KIT)   SKIN   :   REAR   (   )   SCAN

23. KNEE   (TANK)   LAST   :   RAIN   (   )   BEST

24. READ   (PRAY)   PLOY   :   LIAR   (   )   FOOT

25. FIBS   (LIMB)   MALE   :   VERY   (   )   ALTO

Anthem Short Revision Papers
11+ and 12+ Verbal Reasoning Book 1
Answer Sheet 20

Please select your answers by filling in the correct boxes.

Name:

1
- TAPE ☐
- MEAT ☐
- TRAM ☐
- RAPT ☐
- TEAM ☐

2
- GALE ☐
- BLUE ☐
- DUEL ☐
- BALE ☐
- BEAD ☐

3
- STOP ☐
- POST ☐
- LAST ☐
- LOST ☐
- SOOT ☐

4
- TOOK ☐
- COAL ☐
- TALK ☐
- TOOL ☐
- SOAK ☐

5
- BEST ☐
- STAB ☐
- PEAR ☐
- TEAR ☐
- REAP ☐

6
- Small ample ☐
- ample portions ☐
- portions are ☐
- are my ☐
- my choice ☐

7
- The large ☐
- large camel ☐
- camel entered ☐
- entered the ☐
- the cage ☐

8
- Aunt Ada ☐
- Ada shouted ☐
- shouted very ☐
- very loudly ☐
- loudly and ☐

9
- The advertisements ☐
- advertisements on ☐
- on the ☐
- the television ☐
- television are ☐

10
- is always ☐
- always true ☐
- true if ☐
- if logic ☐
- logic is ☐

11
- D ☐
- T ☐
- L ☐
- B ☐
- M ☐

12
- T ☐
- N ☐
- R ☐
- G ☐
- S ☐

13
- T ☐
- G ☐
- L ☐
- R ☐
- D ☐

14
- A ☐
- E ☐
- B ☐
- O ☐
- S ☐

15
- C ☐
- D ☐
- K ☐
- T ☐
- G ☐

16
- anxious ☐
- discipline ☐
- hesitant ☐
- worried ☐
- apprehensive ☐

17
- commence ☐
- start ☐
- begin ☐
- cease ☐
- race ☐

18
- conceal ☐
- army ☐
- camouflage ☐
- disguise ☐
- divulge ☐

19
- dwelling ☐
- house ☐
- apartment ☐
- furniture ☐
- occupy ☐

20
- comprise ☐
- section ☐
- part ☐
- fraction ☐
- whole ☐

21
- 28 ☐
- 29 ☐
- 31 ☐
- 32 ☐
- 33 ☐

22
- 4 ☐
- 6 ☐
- 8 ☐
- 10 ☐
- 12 ☐

23
- 25 ☐
- 26 ☐
- 27 ☐
- 28 ☐
- 29 ☐

24
- 158 ☐
- 160 ☐
- 162 ☐
- 164 ☐
- 166 ☐

25
- 98 ☐
- 99 ☐
- 101 ☐
- 112 ☐
- 115 ☐

Short Revision Paper 20

In the following questions there should be two groups of three words. The three on the right go together in the same way as the three on the left. Find the missing word, and mark it down on your answer sheet.

1.	COAT	(TAKE)	KEEP	:	PART	( )	AMAZE
2.	SAND	(SNOW)	BLOW	:	BALD	( )	GLUE
3.	CLUE	(LEND)	SAND	:	ALSO	( )	POST
4.	SLOT	(CAST)	PACT	:	LOOK	( )	CATS
5.	BACK	(CRAB)	RAKE	:	BASE	( )	TRIP

In each of the following questions, there is a word of four letters hidden at the end of one word and the beginning of the next. Find the pair of words that contains the hidden word, and mark this pair on your answer sheet.

6. Small ample portions are my choice.

7. The large camel entered the cage.

8. Aunt Ada shouted very loudly and often.

9. The advertisements on the television are persuasive.

10. It is always true if logic is used.

In the following questions, one letter ends the first word in each pair and begins the second. The same letter must be used in both sets of brackets. Mark the correct answer on the answer sheet.

11.	HIN	( )	IME	STAR	( )	ONE
12.	BEE	( )	EAR	FA	( )	AFT
13.	BOL	( )	ONE	CA	( )	IVE
14.	INT	( )	VER	HER	( )	PEN
15.	SIN	( )	ONE	WIN	( )	REAT

In the following questions, two words do not fit with the other three. What are the two odd ones out? Mark them on the answer sheet.

16.   anxious discipline hesitant worried apprehensive

17.   commence start begin cease race

18.   conceal army camouflage disguise divulge

19.   dwelling house apartment furniture occupy

20.   comprise section part fraction whole

In the following questions, find the number that completes the series in the best way, and mark it down on the answer sheet.

21.   3 5 9 15 23 _____

22.   8 12 6 10 4 8 2 _____

23.   41 38 36 33 31 28 _____

24.   2 6 18 54 _____

25.   7 8 15 23 38 61 _____

Paper 7 Answers

1. 28
2. 5
3. 248
4. 58
5. 10
6. UTQB
7. TMFQU
8. ETLRP
9. SCREW
10. IZUDE
11. Fred
12. Tony
13. Tom
14. Jim
15. Harry
16. yearly & annually
17. valour & bravery
18. terror & fear
19. reveal & show
20. remedy & cure
21. C
22. E
23. B
24. A
25. B

Paper 8 Answers

1. SUNLIGHT
2. TABLECLOTH
3. WAISTCOAT
4. ACTOR
5. NOTHING
6. REAPER
7. ECHO
8. EASE
9. DEED
10. PERT
11. TIE
12. SEA
13. RAIN
14. SCORE
15. PAIN
16. 40
17. 2
18. 76
19. 50
20. 70
21. air on
22. pie rarely
23. the missing
24. cream are
25. races cars

Paper 9 Answers

1. vague & clear
2. liberty & captivity
3. empty & full
4. refuse & approve
5. steep & flat
6. trap & edit
7. house & empty
8. modern & guilty
9. car & yacht
10. punctual & rigid
11. 29
12. 1080
13. 40
14. 216
15. 13
16. T
17. T
18. S
19. E
20. U
21. RO
22. PQ
23. RY
24. VZ
25. YZ

Paper 10 Answers

1. BELOW
2. OVERTURN
3. CARPET
4. NIGHTFALL
5. NECKLACE
6. FIND
7. JETTY
8. WAR
9. RID
10. MICE
11. shrink & diminish
12. jealous & envious
13. boast & brag
14. courage & bravery
15. still & motionless
16. break
17. firm
18. gap
19. kind
20. mount
21. H
22. T
23. B
24. O
25. Y

Paper 11 Answers

1. TRY & ATTEMPT
2. WALK & STROLL
3. MEET & ASSEMBLE
4. KEEP & RETAIN
5. DOUBTFUL & UNCERTAIN
6. ACT
7. AND
8. RUM
9. LIP
10. LAY
11. ten & hundred
12. thin & small
13. construct & demolish
14. front & top
15. note & word
16. 47
17. 12
18. 18
19. 60
20. 4
21. R
22. R
23. R
24. R
25. T

Paper 12 Answers

1. KHES
2. ITKF
3. BPTQKFC
4. TKJR
5. NYWEJQ
6. 16
7. 11
8. 53
9. 14
10. 33
11. NOWHERE
12. INSURE
13. INCOME
14. PACKAGE
15. PASSPORT
16. on certain
17. reach inside
18. the meat
19. shave in
20. teachers hopping
21. D
22. B
23. D
24. C
25. A

Answers to Short Revision Papers

Paper 1 Answers

1. seaweed
2. carton
3. season
4. washer
5. target
6. Come and
7. blame attached
8. from India
9. cover your
10. post operative
11. U
12. K
13. T
14. P
15. LM
16. male
17. deal
18. rate
19. lead
20. rule
21. D
22. E
23. E
24. C
25. C

Paper 2 Answers

1. RAPID
2. FRONT
3. GROWS
4. WORD
5. SEA
6. 15
7. 91
8. 2
9. 42
10. 3
11. AD
12. I
13. I
14. R
15. R
16. 8
17. 32
18. 11
19. 23
20. 45
21. foggy & misty
22. part & fraction
23. cherish & love
24. convict & prisoner
25. forgive & pardon

Paper 3 Answers

1. conflagration & hurricane
2. enormous & huge
3. sorrow & failure
4. doubt & knowledge
5. calendar & clock
6. l
7. w
8. s
9. b
10. t
11. slam
12. seat
13. idea
14. most
15. kerb
16. large & massive
17. light & buoyant
18. extended & enlarged
19. begin & commence
20. soft & gentle
21. HV
22. UZ
23. OK
24. DC
25. WS

Paper 4 Answers

1. Tom
2. David
3. hockey
4. John
5. Harry
6. adjust
7. cheer
8. point
9. draw
10. even
11. SPACE
12. CASES
13. PEARS
14. CAPES
15. PACES
16. ALL
17. LAY
18. EAT
19. PAD
20. AND
21. game & whistle
22. bees & wolves
23. trunk & leaf
24. sock & foot
25. clock & watch

Paper 5 Answers

1. cure
2. foam
3. stall
4. sane
5. mint
6. PAGE
7. ANTS
8. ART
9. APE
10. ARE
11. 47
12. 10
13. 61
14. 25
15. 28
16. station & terminus
17. calm & straight
18. ears & tongue
19. brick & snow
20. watch & listen
21. DRAB
22. TEST
23. HELM
24. GILT
25. PART

Paper 6 Answers

1. N
2. A
3. T
4. I
5. T
6. Y
7. H
8. S
9. T
10. T
11. QR
12. HJ
13. WR
14. SZ
15. BE
16. joyful & miserable
17. expensive & cheap
18. command & obey
19. miniature & giant
20. pardon & condemn
21. bus and
22. top layer
23. stolen diamond
24. top almost
25. bus ended

Paper 13 Answers

1. prison & punishment
2. medal & fearful
3. noisy & order
4. circus & clown
5. house & abode
6. COW
7. ROW
8. ARK
9. MAN
10. LOW
11. 63
12. 20
13. 240
14. 25
15. 29
16. PALACE
17. HIDDEN
18. PEASANT
19. ROTATE
20. GRIMACE
21. H
22. K
23. S
24. R
25. C

Paper 14 Answers

1. agree
2. alone
3. awkward
4. back
5. blow
6. DROWN
7. PEAT
8. XTTAWT
9. EBZCT
10. XDZQD
11. K
12. P
13. E
14. BP
15. MG
16. 45
17. 19
18. 6
19. 8
20. 20
21. BAT
22. CAT
23. BATS
24. DONE
25. LUMP

Paper 15 Answers

1. bolt
2. glare
3. hit
4. mount
5. trip
6. G
7. D
8. B
9. L
10. B
11. ROUT
12. TOUR
13. SORT
14. RUST
15. OUST
16. book & music
17. four & three
18. centimetre & decade
19. rein & hear
20. bad & gigantic
21. RT
22. KP
23. KH
24. YZ
25. WC

Paper 16 Answers

1. L
2. R
3. A
4. E
5. H
6. 40
7. 70
8. 8
9. 11
10. 16
11. L
12. U
13. P
14. MK
15. JE
16. tooth & person
17. sight & sound
18. sweet & sour
19. whole & stake
20. liquid & solid
21. teacher or
22. The advert
23. Some alloys
24. orange are
25. was his

Paper 17 Answers

1. gloom
2. catch
3. cool
4. jam
5. scale
6. portable
7. ransack
8. carton
9. inlet
10. cannon
11. DIE
12. COIL
13. HORN
14. LIT
15. CLAP
16. MEAL
17. PAST
18. PORT
19. CARE
20. SOAK
21. 30
22. 72
23. 5
24. 30
25. 55

Paper 18 Answers

1. HAT
2. OIL
3. RUM
4. TRY
5. CAT
6. football & play
7. bike & plane
8. glass & wood
9. soar & dear
10. often & surprise
11. 13
12. 63
13. 35
14. 126
15. 2
16. U
17. C
18. L
19. E
20. G
21. display & reveal
22. hoard & save
23. oppose & resist
24. command & instruction
25. presence & attendance

Paper 19 Answers

1. calamity & disaster
2. calm & peaceful
3. dissolve & melt
4. frown & scowl
5. misery & sadness
6. NM
7. V
8. I
9. Y
10. QY
11. M
12. N
13. P
14. N
15. M
16. PANS
17. PAIN
18. SPIN
19. SPAN
20. PINS
21. CHIN
22. CAR
23. TEAR
24. FLAT
25. TEAR

Paper 20 Answers

1. TRAM
2. BLUE
3. LOST
4. TALK
5. STAB
6. Small ample
7. camel entered
8. Ada shouted
9. The advertisements
10. if logic
11. T
12. R
13. D
14. O
15. G
16. discipline & hesitant
17. cease & race
18. army & divulge
19. furniture & occupy
20. comprise & whole
21. 33
22. 6
23. 26
24. 162
25. 99